Catholic History

A Captivating Guide to the History of the Catholic Church, Starting with the Teachings of Jesus Christ Through the Roman Empire and Middle Ages to the Present

Free Bonus from Captivating History
(Available for a Limited time)

Hi History Lovers!

Now you have a chance to join our exclusive history list so you can get your first history ebook for free as well as discounts and a potential to get more history books for free! Simply visit the link below to join.

Also, make sure to follow us on Facebook, Twitter and Youtube by searching for Captivating History.

Contents

Introduction

The Catholic Church can trace its history two thousand years ago, which makes it the oldest institution in the Western world. Its beginnings lay with Jesus Christ and a small nucleus of his followers. This faith spread quickly through the Roman Empire and was shaped by Roman culture, society, and politics. Faith in Jesus and his resurrection was almost exterminated by the Roman emperors' persecutions. Many Christians perished once they refused to conform to the empire's politics. But these persecutions served only to magnify the spirit of the faithful, and the spread of Christianity continued, despite the savage fury of the state. Finally, Christianity won against the ancient paganism when Emperor Constantine the Great was drawn to its side. In 312, he adorned his army with the symbol of Christ and led his soldiers to a victory that secured not only the unity of the divided empire but also religious freedom for all Christians.

Since the beginning of the Christian faith, its destiny has been linked to the state. But the church proved it could continue living without the state once the Western Roman Empire fell to the barbarians. During those dark times of the Middle Ages, Christianity proved it could be a beacon to the faithful. It proudly stood as the only power that could resist the barbarians. Under the leadership of strong individuals such as Pope Gregory the Great, the church asserted its spirituality to the barbarians and converted them to Christianity. Finally, a new Christian civilization was born in the west, commonly known as Christendom.

For the next thousand years, the church would be responsible for the public and individual life of Christendom. It brought about laws, institutions, culture, tradition, architecture, and a belief system. The popes managed to establish their authority over the whole western secular world, but when they tried to do the same with the Christian Church, it fell apart. The Western and Eastern Churches would never again reconcile. Nevertheless, the magnificent medieval popes, perhaps best epitomized in Innocent III, controlled the Western Church, as well as the moral and social lives of kings, queens, knights, monks, nuns, peasants, and merchants.

Papal authority started deteriorating with the approach of modern times. The Renaissance and its ideas of critical thinking brought new social, religious, economic, and cultural tides that undermined the Christian unity of the Western world. Martin Luther openly denied papal authority and started a revolution, which would eventually lead to the collapse of the Catholic bureaucracy and theocracy. Nevertheless, the church in Rome managed to save itself by instituting very thorough reforms, which were promulgated by the Council of Trent. The reforms surprisingly didn't reduce the influence of the church on the everyday life of people and their faith. Instead, it was intensified and even rejuvenated by the establishment of various religious orders.

However, the rationalism and liberalism of the 17th century created another spiritual crisis, and the church grimly decided to assume a defensive position against all the trends of the modern secular world. Even throughout events such as the French Revolution, the church managed to keep itself unchanged and its faith undeterred. Yet another spiritual revival followed that involved an even greater expansion of the Christian faith, this time in the newly discovered Americas. However, the attitude the Catholic Church had toward modernity remained unchanged. Pius IX summarized this negative and condemnatory attitude in his *Syllabus of Errors*, an encyclical that condemned the idea of liberal secularism. The church even entered the 20th century despising technological and scientific innovations.

But the next generation of popes, those who grew up and started serving in an ever-changing and developing world, displayed a progressive way of thinking and leadership. They even enhanced the prestige of the Catholic Church with the reforms introduced by the Second Vatican Council, which had been summoned by Pope John XXIII in 1962. Although he died just a year later, the progressive changes couldn't be stopped. A dialog with the whole world was opened, and the church sought ways to repair its relationship with the secular states. These reforms are still being implemented and discussed. The church is changing slowly but steadily, with modern popes refusing to condemn such things as artificial insemination or even the LGBTQ community.

Chapter 1 – Jesus Christ

According to Saint John, Jesus Christ is the eternal Son of the Father because his nature is divine. His purpose is the preservation of the world. But the Son of God also has a human nature in which he is simply Jesus of Nazareth. As such, his purpose is to symbolize the religious growth of humanity. Thus, Jesus has a dual nature, a divine one and a human one. When unified in one person, these natures create the perfect man, the ideal of virtue and piety. He is both the Son and Lord, made of our human flesh and blood but is also the Holy Spirit. Jesus Christ is the perfect link between humans and their heavenly creator. The Son of God died to redeem humanity, and in doing so, he started a new future in which he is the head of the church. That is why the modern Catholic Church regards Jesus Christ as the founder of their church, which is his body.

Jesus Christ didn't write anything himself, but his disciples did. And they didn't only write about his ideas and religious teachings but also his life story. The two natures (divine and human) of Jesus are perfectly combined in his biographies, satisfying both historians and his religious followers. It is spectacular to observe how he managed to grow gradually and so humanly despite his holy nature. He lived in a human world and had to bow to human laws, which would only serve to advance his wisdom and stature. But it was also through his completely human life that Jesus showed people a path everyone could take to achieve perfection and personal salvation.

Jesus Christ was born in Bethlehem in Judea sometime between 6 BCE and 6 CE. It is widely believed that he was born during the reign of the first Roman emperor, Caesar Augustus (63 BCE-14 CE). We know little to nothing about the childhood of Jesus Christ, but there are apocryphal gospels that try to fill the void. They attempt to paint a picture of a childhood so perfect and pure, one without sin and completely holy, yet natural and human. The result was an unnatural child who spoke to animals and to whom all of nature bowed. But the truth is that Jesus Christ's youth is a mystery, and we know of only one instance from his childhood. When he was twelve years old, Jesus astonished the doctors in the Temple by questioning them and answering their questions with much wisdom. But even while doing so, Jesus remained humble and respective to his elders, evoking reverence and awe in them. It is believed that Jesus was a quiet child and that he often went unnoticed. He grew up in the mountain village of Nazareth in the region of Galilee with no schools or teachers. He had only the nature around him, the Old Testament, the services of the local synagogue, and his own communion with God to lead and shape him into what he was to become.

Jesus started his public mission only after he turned thirty years old, after he was inaugurated as the Messiah by baptism, which was performed by John the Baptist. But his public work lasted for only three years. It is in these three years that the deepest meaning of the history of the Christian religion is condensed.

Jesus was a Jew, and he was introduced to Jewish teachings. His teachings never left the sphere of Jewish beliefs, but he expanded on them and gave them a new meaning. From the start, Jesus was aware of his divinity and himself as the king of Israel. But he claimed his kingdom was not in this world but the spiritual one. He chose twelve apostles, who were also Jews, and seventy Gentile disciples (Gentiles do not practice the Jewish faith). They were all common people, illiterate fishermen, and field workers. Jesus didn't choose scholars and leaders, nor did he preach to wealthy and powerful individuals. His world revolved around the low-born, of sinners, thieves, and betrayers. The lower class of society was neglected and despised by the mighty leaders. They were at the bottom of society, and Jesus wanted to raise them high and show them how to lead noble lives.

Jesus traveled through Palestine and through the towns and villages north of the Sea of Galilee, teaching with power and authority that gave him the people's unconditional obedience and love. He had no previous training on how to teach, and he had to rely on his intuition and experience to shape the minds of his disciples. He spoke the words of life and wisdom, and he performed various miracles, which only served to display the might and glory of his heavenly Father. The miracles he performed were all supernatural, yet they fit the historical concept of his existence. To Christians, these miracles are symbols and signs of how the spirit and mind are superior to the human body and how divine grace is superior to human nature. Their significance is purely symbolic, and as practical proof of his doctrine, they were simply called his "works." Jesus also prophesied his martyrdom to his disciples.

The culmination of Christ's mission came with his entrance into the city of Jerusalem. By this time, he already had a reputation of being a political and religious agitator, especially among the Romans.

Everything we know about Jesus and his life comes from the Gospels, which were written by the Four Evangelists—Mark, Mathew, Luke, and John. The main goal of the Gospels wasn't to record a biographical and historically accurate account of Jesus's life but to persuade readers of his divine nature. This non-historical character of the Gospels can be easily observed due to significant differences in the details of Christ's life. Sometimes, these details are even contradictory. The first contradiction can be seen right at the beginning of the Gospels of Matthew and John, as they dated his birth differently. While Mathew believed Jesus was born during the reign of King Herod of Judea, which would put the birth occurring sometime in 6 BCE, John wrote that Jesus was born during the period when Quirinius served as legate of Syria. This would mean Jesus was born somewhere between 6 BCE and 6 CE. Although the Gospels disagree on many details, their theological message remains the same: Jesus Christ was the long-awaited Messiah who was to bring salvation to both Jews and Gentiles.

The Gospels were written some forty years (some even say seventy years) after the death of Jesus Christ. Their authors never claimed to know the life of their Messiah. They simply wrote down what was left in the collective memory of the Christian communities. Because the authors were free of obligations to follow Jesus's life historically, they could include stories and episodes of dubious authenticity. They even dared to put words in the mouth of their Messiah to bring the doctrine of faith closer to the people. The authors of the Gospels never tried to answer the questions a modern Christian might wonder, such as what Jesus looked like or how he sounded. Instead, they tried to capture the essence of the faith he represented and preached. This is why some scholars try to divide Jesus into a historical figure and one based on the Gospels.

The main message of the Gospels is the same message Jesus conveyed to his disciples and followers, that the Kingdom of Heaven had arrived and that it was time for all to repent. The main goal of Jesus Christ was to persuade the people of the urgency to repent for their past sins and to start living their lives following God's will. To achieve this, he didn't exclude the most devious sinners. He didn't believe that the repenting of sins was allowed only to those who were good people or who had religious knowledge. His message included all of humanity because God was good.

But Christ didn't only preach the love of God and what was good about the faith. He was aware that suffering existed regardless of how devoted to the faith one was. Thus, he claimed that in suffering and anguish, a man could come closer to God. Humans do not need to comprehend evil and its efforts to sway people away from God. They only needed faith in their heavenly Father, who they would join in death.

Suffering and agony came to be seen as desirable among the followers of Christ. No one should invoke suffering, but if one was presented with it, they should embrace it. Suffering helped people join the heavenly kingdom, so poverty, bereavement, and hunger were seen as a path to that kingdom. They were no longer the ultimate evil as they had been in the past. Now money, greed, and the absence of love were the things one should be wary of.

Jesus also preached love, not only the love of the heavenly Father toward his children on earth but also love between humans. He regarded the love people had for each other as the ultimate celebration of God's love for humanity. In the scene where he is greeted by a harlot in the home of a Pharisee who kissed and washed his feet with her tears and dried them with her hair, Jesus explains how even sinners can love and are deserving of God's affection. By washing Jesus's feet and expressing her love for him, the harlot proved she was aware of how much she had sinned and how much forgiveness she needed. According to the Bible, those who express love will be forgiven, and those who show only a little love will receive only a little forgiveness.

For Jesus, love was above the law. In fact, many of his messages were contradictory to the human and religious laws of Judea. He often preached to his pupils not to rely on human laws but to invoke their own religious experiences and perform the deeds that God inspired them to do. In the name of his faith, Jesus often criticized and even attacked rigorous Jewish traditions, such as observing the Sabbath. He belittled the temples and challenged the establishment. In turn, the temples, the law, and the empire had to react.

Aware that his end was nearing, Jesus gathered his followers for one last meal together. This event is remembered in the history of Christianity as the Last Supper. Such gatherings were nothing new among Jesus's disciples, as they often shared their meals and celebrated their love for God. This type of communal gathering was also already established in the Jewish tradition and was not Christ's invention. But the Messiah did add a new aspect to it. During the meal, he offered bread and wine to his guests, claiming they were receiving his body and his blood. He also asked the disciples to continue practicing the communal consumption of bread and wine in remembrance of Jesus's passion and suffering. Thus, he created the tradition that would translate into communion, which is practiced in the Christian faith. Jesus explained that by consuming his body and blood, his followers would confirm his sacrifice, which would establish a new covenant between God and humans.

That same night, Jesus was arrested by both Jewish and Roman authorities. This means that both religious and political motives were behind his arrest. The Jewish leaders believed Christ was yet another Messiah-pretender who preached that God's kingdom would come through political revolt. They feared that Jesus would bring down the wrath of the Roman Empire onto the people of Judea, and they wanted to prevent the brutal repressions the Romans would install. They also couldn't forget that Jesus spoke against the Temple and criticized their religious laws. In the eyes of the Jewish leaders, Christ was a heretic, and he used blasphemy to avert the people from the one true faith.

Pontius Pilate, a Roman governor of Judea, believed Jesus was innocent of plotting a political revolt. He wanted to set Jesus free, as he saw no tangible evidence against him. But the Jewish authorities pressed Pilate and threatened to report the governor to the Roman emperor. Scared for his position, Pontius Pilate gave in to the pressure and had Jesus executed.

However, historically, it is unlikely that the events occurred as described in the Gospels. Many scholars believe that Jesus Christ represented a true political danger to the Roman authorities and that this was the only reason for his arrest and execution. They even go as far as to say that the Gospels, which were written by early Christians, completely exonerate the Romans to please them and to avoid their wrath.

Jesus was crucified, as was the custom in the ancient Roman Empire, but the morning after his death, something strange happened. This event is described in all of the Gospels, as well as in the Acts of the Apostles and various other religious texts. Jesus was resurrected, and he also communicated with his disciples and the women who came to tend to his grave.

This event is complicated for historians. All the sources that describe the resurrection differ from each other, and they cannot agree to whom and where Jesus first appeared after the resurrection. Historical criticism makes this specific event somewhat more believable by explaining how each Christian community relates to the resurrection differently. Through the story of Christ's resurrection, each of these communities had the chance to reflect on their theological conceptions, morality, and local associations.

But in the end, modern scholars don't really question if the resurrection occurred or not. Real or fictional, it had a great impact on modern Christian society and on the collective memory of all Christians. Instead of questioning it, scholars try to reconstruct the sequence of events.

The final consensus is that Mary Magdalene went to the tomb of Jesus on the morning of the first Easter. She saw that the stone that had been blocking the entrance to the tomb was moved. Fearing robbers had entered the holy site, she ran to Saint Peter and notified him about what had happened. Peter entered the opened tomb and found it empty except for the burial cloth lying on the ground. When he rushed to the disciples to tell them the body was missing, Jesus appeared to Peter.

Chapter 2 – The Apostolic Age

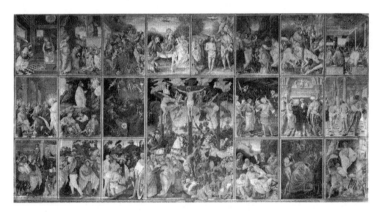

Church fresco from 1513, Gaudenzio Ferrari, Church of Santa Maria Delle Grazie, Italy.
https://en.wikipedia.org/wiki/Christianity_in_the_1st_century#/media/File:GaudenzioFerra ri_StorieCristo_Varallo2.jpg

The Christian faith started when Jesus was resurrected. Before that, Jesus was regarded as the Messiah of an already existing faith, Judaism. But early Christianity wasn't anything like we know it in the modern day. It was still just a branch of Judaism, and their followers were members of an apocalyptic messianic Jewish sect. Resurrection was not a new concept in Judaism, which is why early Christians didn't see themselves as followers of a different faith. They only thought that Jesus's resurrection gave a new meaning and clarity to their religious sentiment. Jesus did everything in accordance with the ancient Jewish scriptures, and Saint Paul lets the Corinthians know this. In his First Epistle to the Corinthians, he says that Jesus died for the sins of humanity. He also says that, per the Scriptures, Jesus was resurrected.

If Christianity started with the resurrection of Jesus Christ, then the first Christian church started with the Pentecostal explosion of the Holy Spirit, which filled everyone with the confirmation of their faith. They were also filled with the need to spread their faith to nonbelievers. Pentecost first occurred when the apostles and other followers of Jesus gathered in Jerusalem to celebrate a Jewish harvest feast known as the Feast of Weeks. The apostles took the opportunity of the celebration to obey the command of their Lord and repeat his words and acts. Thus, they prayed and shared bread and wine, which were his body and blood that he sacrificed for the redemption of humanity. Pentecost is still celebrated, and it takes place fifty days after Easter Sunday.

During his life, Jesus chose twelve of his disciples to be apostles. They were tasked with spreading the Word of God throughout the world. After his death, the twelve apostles remained in Jerusalem, where they continued to lead the community of believers. The leader of the apostles was Peter, named thus by Jesus. Peter means "rock" in Hebrew, and when Jesus changed his name from Simon to Peter, he was recognizing the strength of Simon's faith. Later on, Jesus said he would build his church upon such rocks, meaning many others would come to be as strong in faith as Peter. After all, they would have to carry the weight of the truth on their shoulders. Besides Peter, the apostles were Andrew (Peter's brother), Philip, James (son of Zebedee), John, Matthew, Thomas, Bartholomew, Thaddaeus (also called Judas the Zealot), James (son of Alphaeus), Simon the Zealot, and Judas Iscariot who betrayed Jesus.

After the death of Jesus and before the turn of the century, these twelve apostles went throughout the Roman Empire (and even farther) to preach Christianity. Saint Paul did the same, and he called himself an apostle even though Jesus didn't personally choose him. Nevertheless, "apostle" is Roman for "mission," and since Paul spread the mission, he deserved to bear the title of apostle.

The story of how the chosen disciples of Jesus traveled and managed to found his church in different parts of the known world (the Mediterranean, Africa, the Middle East, and all the way to India) is a remarkable one. But historically, it is hard to follow their path, as there is little to no evidence of their works. Nevertheless, it is possible to reconstruct the basic story of the spread of Christianity, which started from the death of Jesus and lasted until the last of the apostles died in 100 CE. This is why it is called the Apostolic Age.

The Spread of Christianity Through the Empire

It is important to understand that at this point, Christianity was still not a religion on its own. It was a sect within Judaism, and the apostles, therefore, didn't spread a new faith but rather a new thought within the already existing one. The apostles and their followers remained faithful to the Temple and Judaic law. But not all of the Jewish leaders welcomed this new sect and their belief that Jesus was the promised Messiah. Some wanted to suppress them; in their eyes, the Christians were nonconformists. But it wasn't easy to do so because the public supported Christians due to their piety and respect for Jewish customs and laws.

The spread of Christianity wasn't an explosive event. Instead, it occurred gradually. At first, it came to the Jewish communities around the Mediterranean Sea. The apostles who traveled from Jerusalem to spread their faith did so in accordance with Jesus, who claimed he came to preach to the last of the house of Israel. Thus, early Christians believed that the faith should be spread only among Jews.

However, Christianity soon started to be spread among non-Jews. It is believed that this happened because some of the Jewish communities were too Hellenized, and their ties to the Temple and the law were loose. They communicated with the non-Jews in everyday life and spoke about their newfound faith. One leader of these unorthodox Hellenized Jews was Stephen, a deacon of the early Christian Church of Jerusalem. He was arrested for spreading heresy and was put on trial by Jewish authorities. He was sentenced to death by stoning, and he became the first Christian martyr. Today, he is known as Saint Stephen.

Stephen's martyrdom was the start of the general persecution of Christians. And it wasn't only the apostles who were targeted. All the believers in Jerusalem were in danger, and they sought refuge in far-away countries. They took this opportunity to spread the faith wherever they went. When the first Christians reached Antioch, an ancient Greek city in modern-day Turkey, the spread of the church exploded and changed the history of the world. This is where the first Gentiles were baptized, and the faith spread out of the closed Jewish communities. Antioch became the center of Christianity for the Gentiles.

Although the Gentiles were not Jewish, the Christian Church accepted them because it was more liberal than the unorthodox Jewish Temple. The Gentiles who converted to Christianity were exempted from following the Judaic law, and they didn't have to be circumcised.

However, when great numbers of Gentiles started attending the church, some of the Jewish Christians began seeing them as a threat. The traditional-minded Jewish Christians demanded that all Gentiles should obey the law and undergo circumcision. They feared that the great number of Gentiles in the church would make it lose its Jewish character, and this caused the first controversy within the Christian community. This controversy revolved around the question of whether the church should remain exclusively Jewish and remain a sect or if it should spread to encompass all of humanity and become a religion of its own.

The man who resolved this problem was Saul of Tarsus, better known by his Roman name of Paul. He is now regarded as the most important individual of the Apostolic Age. According to the Acts of the Apostles, Paul was one of the early persecutors of Christians. He was sent to Damascus to arrest the followers of Christ and bring them back to Jerusalem to meet justice. But on his travels, Jesus appeared to him and made him blind. Paul's sight was restored by one of Christ's disciples, Ananias of Damascus. Paul soon converted and started spreading the gospel. The New Testament has twenty-seven books, of which fourteen were authored by Saint Paul. These are known as the Pauline epistles. Some of these were probably written by his students in his name, but at least seven of them have been authenticated as being Paul's work.

Saint Paul met with the leaders of the Christian Church (namely Peter, James, and John) and discussed the status of the Gentiles. Paul's opinion was highly regarded at this point, and he was chosen to spread the message among the Gentiles. But Paul did much more than that. To appeal to the non-Jews, he stripped the Gospels of all Jewish characteristics and made it more attractive to everyone. Paul saw Christianity as a liberation from the strict laws of the Jewish faith, and he believed that it was enough to have faith in Jesus in order to receive salvation. In his opinion, obedience to the law was not necessary.

Paul's abandonment of the Judaic law might have been instigated by his personal experience. He was obedient to the law in the days before he converted, and under the law, he persecuted the Christians. Perhaps in the realization of his mistake, he also realized that the strict Jewish law was contradictory to his newfound faith in Jesus.

But this was not the end of the troubles within the church. Even though the meeting in Jerusalem resulted in an agreement that Gentiles should be allowed to practice Christianity, some Jews didn't want to share common meals with them. Even Saint Peter, who mostly agreed with the views of Saint Paul regarding the Gentiles, didn't want to join the common table. Paul confronted Peter in a public dispute known as the incident at Antioch. The result of the confrontation remains uncertain. The Catholics believe that Paul won and that Peter realized his mistake. But some scholars disagree. Paul never claimed victory in his writings, and he soon left Antioch and never returned, as he was unwanted there.

In around 50 CE, the Council of Jerusalem was summoned. It was the first ecumenical council, and the main goal was to resolve the issue of the Gentiles once and for all. Surprisingly, Peter spoke positively about the Gentiles, and he expressed his belief that both Jews and non-Jews were saved through the grace of Jesus. This meant that no matter the differences between them, both groups equally loved and respected the Lord and achieved salvation through Christ. The Council of Jerusalem decided to allow the Gentiles exemption from some Jewish laws, such as circumcision. However, many other questions were raised during the debate, and it was decided that some of the laws had to be obeyed, even by Gentiles, such as not consuming animal blood or engaging in fornication. Thus, the unity of the Christian Church was preserved, and many traditionalists were soothed.

Not all Jewish Christians accepted the decision of the First Council of Jerusalem, and they continued their efforts to bring the Gentiles around and make them obey the Jewish laws. But they were fighting a losing battle. The number of Gentiles was far greater than the traditionalists, and in time, the Jewish Christians became a minority in the church. Paul's interpretation of the Gospels was accepted by the church, and officially, the church was no longer an exclusive Jewish institution. This was the point in Christianity when the church became accepting of all humanity—an important point in history indeed.

Paul was aware that the future of the church lay with the Gentiles, and he rushed to spread his mission around the known world, which consisted of Asia Minor and Greece at the time. His missionary journeys resulted in the foundation of congregations in the cities of Athens, Thessalonica, Corinth, Ephesus, Lystra, and Beroea.

Paul preached only in the towns and cities that Christianity hadn't reached yet. He would start preaching in synagogues to the Jewish community of the city, whom he tried to persuade into believing that Christ was the savior promised in the Old Testament. But more often than not, his preaching to the Jews resulted in trouble. He met the strongest opposition in Corinth, where he spent eighteen months preaching. He had more success with the Gentiles in Corinth than with the Jews, and he managed to find followers there.

Saint Paul wrote many letters to the Christian communities he founded. In these letters, we can see how he shaped the early Christian Church. He wasn't only spreading the gospel; he also organized the internal works of the churches he left behind. In his letters, he wrote about deep theological themes, but he was also concerned with the details of the life of his Christian communities.

Thanks to Saint Paul and his efforts to allow the conversion of the Gentiles, Christianity started spreading rapidly. Around the year 59, Paul wrote that he had exhausted his abilities in the eastern Mediterranean and that he wanted to travel farther west. His new goal was Spain, Rome's oldest mainland province. Spain was the center of Roman life in the western Mediterranean and a perfect spot from where to start spreading Christianity into the Western world.

The Success of Christianity

It is not known if Paul ever reached Spain. He might have gone there but soon turned back to Jerusalem to bring the alms for the poor he had collected. Perhaps he never even arrived in Spain and instead decided to go to Jerusalem directly from Rome. Whatever the case, Paul took the opportunity of Rome to give his final thoughts on the matters of the church's division between the Jews and the Gentiles. He wrote his famous Epistle to the Romans in which he reflected on the problem of the Jewish law against the gospel. He was eager to clear any reservations the Jewish Christians still had toward the Gentiles. He wanted a unified church and the undisturbed spread of the gospel throughout the world. The essence of Paul's belief was later described in the Epistle to the Ephesians, which was probably written by one of his disciples at a later point. In it, he expresses his thought of "One Lord, one faith, one baptism"; in other words, a perfectly unified church.

But while in Jerusalem, Paul was recognized by some of the Jews, who saw him as a threat to their faith. They accused him of betrayal and demanded his life. The Roman Tribune arrested Paul, thus saving his life. Although he was safe, he had to spend the next two years in prison. Paul appealed to Roman Emperor Nero, who managed to transfer him to Rome and place him under house arrest to await his trial, which wouldn't take place for two more years.

Rome then raised another accusation against Paul. They needed Paul as a scapegoat for the troubles Rome had with the Christians. Pagan Rome couldn't allow the spread of the new, uniform version of Judaism because it was a threat to the Roman social order. Paul was eventually sentenced to death in Rome and was beheaded. Legend has it that his head bounced three times. Each time it touched the earth, a spring was formed. This is why the church raised on the presumed spot of Paul's execution is named "St Paul at the Three Fountains."

There were many other missionaries of Christianity who were equally enthusiastic about spreading their faith. Unfortunately, we know little to nothing about them. Even the tales of other apostles are mostly legends dated to the 2nd century CE. According to these legends, Saint Andrew evangelized the Scythians, Thomas the Parthians, and Bartholomew traveled to India and South Arabia. The only thing we can conclude for certain is that many missionaries preached the gospel across the vast Roman Empire. By the end of the 1st century CE, Christianity was a well-established faith.

The Jewish Christians didn't have as much luck in spreading the faith to their Jewish compatriots as the Gentiles did. The Jews stubbornly resisted Christianity and even announced an official censure of it around 85 CE. But the point that marks the emergence of Christianity as a separate religion took place in 70 CE. This was when the Romans destroyed Jerusalem and its temple complex. The trouble began in 66 when the Jews revolted against Roman dominion. In turn, the emperor sent his army to deal with the disobedient Jews. The destruction of the Temple prompted Christians to blame the Jews. They considered that Jewish stubbornness and refusal to accept Jesus as the Messiah had brought down the destruction of Jerusalem. The rejection of Judaism now became essential for the Christian existence, and the Jewish Christians found themselves alone, with no support to their cause. Their branch of Christianity eventually disappeared.

Christianity, on the other hand, spread like wildfire among the pagans. The great success of the gospel is a phenomenon that is hard to explain, but it revolutionized the religious thought of the time and made it one of the greatest events of history. The spread of Christianity was made possible by the political, social, and cultural currents of the 1st and 2nd centuries CE. But how and why it was so successful depends much on the philosophical and religious views of the scholars who attempt to explain it.

To understand it from a historical point, one must look at the advantages that the Roman Empire brought to the Mediterranean world. The Romans expanded their empire from the Euphrates River (modern-day Syria) to the Thames River (England) and from the Danube in the north to the Sahara Desert in the south. It took them four centuries to complete the conquest of the then known world. The empire bound together many different peoples, cultures, and social orders. They didn't speak the same language and were of various ethnicities, but they all suddenly found themselves connected through trade. They were different, yet they were all part of one great empire.

This connection of the people served the first Christian missionaries greatly. They could easily travel through the empire and spread their gospel. The Romans encouraged people to move and mingle because they wanted to create an imperial cultural hegemony of all its citizens based on Hellenism. This meant that Rome promoted a common language that would bind the people even tighter together. This language was Greek, and the Christians could use it to be understood almost anywhere in the Roman Empire. Another thing that helped the Christians move around the empire and spread their faith was the relative peace that was in place at the time. This was due to the efforts of Emperor Augustus, who defeated Mark Antony and Cleopatra around 31 CE and established a sole rule. The stable form of government he brought to Rome ensured the easy defeat of the empire's enemies and a great deal of peace. Only the barbaric tribes to the north posed some menace to Rome, but they didn't affect the Christians' efforts to spread their religion.

The peace and the increasing prosperity of the Roman Empire's citizens brought about a period of laid-back enjoyment of life. Theaters, amphitheaters, stadiums, various games, plays, celebrations, and ceremonies left people amused but also spiritually hungry. The rapid social changes left many people confused, and the loss of political freedom made the Roman citizens search for a new purpose. It didn't help that the successors of Caesar Augustus were a very peculiar lot. Among them were famous emperors such as Tiberius, Caligula, Claudius, and Nero. Their court lives were full of intrigue, betrayal, and murder. These were the important figures to whom Roman citizens looked up, and they didn't have much to offer. Tiberius lost his nerve because of the premature death of his son; Caligula was a deranged megalomaniac who wished to be worshiped as a god; Claudius was of weak body and mind, and he allowed his wife Agrippina to manipulate and finally poison him; and finally, there was Nero, who established a rule of terror and who took many lives of the prominent Roman citizens. Under the reign of these Roman emperors, the morale of the people started to decline.

The general atmosphere in the empire was one of doom and pessimism, and this can be seen in the art of the period, especially in the writings of Tacitus, a Roman historian. In such conditions, whichever religion showed up would be able to fill the spiritual vacuum many people felt. The old Roman religion was of no help to spiritually starving nations. Emperors often deified themselves, and the common people could not bring themselves to worship such twisted minds. There was no revival for the pagan faith of Rome, and only a new religion could lift the spirits of the people. Perhaps it was pure luck that Christianity came precisely at this moment.

But Christianity wasn't the only religion that showed up at this crucial moment in history. Many other mystery religions were active, and they rivaled the Christian mission. These mysterious religions were syncretic in nature, often combining the old Hellenistic belief system with new Oriental philosophical thought. Some of the prominent mysteries that were just as popular as Christianity in ancient Rome were the Eleusinian Mysteries (near Athens), the cult of Osiris and Isis from Egypt, and the religion of Great Mother Cybele from Asia Minor. These religious cults were called mysteries because their central rites were kept secret from all but their participants. These mysteries were very different from each other, as well as Christianity. But at one point, they all shared common beliefs, such as the need for a superior deity and a figure who would redeem the people for their sins and bring salvation. This was very much like the Christian philosophy of the time.

Many scholars believe that Christianity was just another mystery that circulated around the empire at the time, as it derived many of its rituals and ceremonies from other religions. But there is no connection between rituals such as baptism, anointment, washing, and sharing meals and what the mysteries practiced.

The most important difference between Christianity and the mysteries of the ancient world rests in the concept of salvation. While the mysteries regarded salvation as a sort of magical freedom from the earthly flesh, Christianity recognized the importance of suffering, sin, and free will. There was no magic involved; rather, it was up to the individual's willingness to suffer and be redeemed for their sins. Also, while the mysteries were deeply rooted in the timeless rhythm of nature, Christianity had its origin in a historical figure, Jesus, which made it more relatable and real.

Ultimately, Christianity owes its success to the love it preached. Many pagans were attracted to the new religion because they saw how connected the Christians were and how much love they had for each other. The Christians devoted themselves not only to the rich but also to the workers, slaves, sinners, prisoners, soldiers, travelers, orphans, widows, and anyone in peril and need. Christianity had a morally higher ground, but it didn't boast about it. It was a religion of peace and love. Many converted pagans, among them philosophers Tatian and Justin, admitted that they were attracted to Christianity because of its morals.

Chapter 3 – The Authority of the Church

The Crucifixion of St. Peter, first bishop of Rome, Caravaggio (1601).
https://en.wikipedia.org/wiki/Saint_Peter#/media/File:Crucifixion_of_Saint_Peter-Caravaggio_(c.1600).jpg

Alongside the spread of Christianity, the church underwent many changes. During the 2nd century CE, it evolved into an institution with a well-defined system of hierarchy, which was based on the sacred texts. The Christian Church of the 2nd century came to resemble the modern-day Catholic Church, with authorities such as bishops, priests, and deacons. But how the church underwent this transformation is one of the most controversial questions in the history of Christianity.

The first Christians were well aware that they belonged to a tightly knit community. They were still part of Judaism, but they had a very distinct identity that separated them from other Jews. They believed that Jesus had been resurrected, which gave them a sense of uniqueness. This can be seen in the names by which they referred to their community: New Israel, the Church of God, and the true remnant of Israel.

All Christians believed that the church was a gift given to humanity by God. Their sense of community and belonging was a miraculous act of the Holy Spirit. Saint Paul reinforced this belief of the supernatural origin of the church. He described it as a new Eve, a wife of Jesus, or as Christ's body or a garden that was watered by the apostles and his followers.

The early church was very much oriented toward Jesus Christ, and this can be seen in its two most important rituals: the Eucharist and baptism. The Eucharist repeats Jesus's words at the Last Supper and his sharing of the bread and wine. This rite has a series of meanings attached to it, from sharing Christ's body and blood to the proclamation of his Second Coming. Baptism was the rite in which one is cleansed of past sins by water. This rite was (and still is in some sects) essential for one's acceptance into the Christian community.

The rites the early church practiced were symbols of the people's unity with Christ and God. But they were not signs of the church's organization. Jesus had organized the church by appointing the twelve apostles, who then had the authority to become the leaders after his death. As time passed and more followers joined the Christian community, this early belief in the authority of the church wasn't enough. The church had to reorganize itself and adapt to the political and social trends. Eventually, the church settled on a three-tiered structure consisting of a bishop, priest, and deacon. This organization of authority was the most conducive to the Christian mission, which explains its wide acceptance.

The first person to talk about the organization of the church is Saint Paul. In his words, "And God has placed in the church first of all apostles, second prophets, third teachers, then miracles, then gifts of healing, of helping, of guidance, and of different kinds of tongues" (1 Corinthians 12:28). According to Paul, the church was founded by Jesus but on the apostolic ministry. They had the authority, and they demanded the obedience of their followers. But they never acted alone; instead, they relied on the fellowship of the whole Christian community. Paul also believed in the constant connection apostles had with each other, as well as the connection any church had with Jerusalem. Thus, he believed that Jerusalem had primacy among the churches and that it could act as the "Mother Church." But above even the churches and the apostles was the gospel. It was the thing that mattered the most, and no one had authority over it. It belonged to everyone, and it was everyone's to share.

But Paul's vision of church authority wasn't long-living. It relied on apostles, who were mortals, and on the immediate end of the world and the Second Coming of Jesus. But when all the apostles died, it became obvious that the church would continue to love and that the end of the world was yet to come. The church found itself at a crossroads where many decisions needed to be made.

The most important among them was how to stay in touch with its origins and how to preserve the unity and continuity of the community and faith without the original apostles. Because the witnesses of Jesus were no longer alive, there was a real danger of people wrongfully interpreting the meaning of Jesus's life and teachings. To avoid this, the church had to come up with a three-fold solution: the establishment of a special ministry, the issuing of a dogmatic list of religious writings, and the creation of a system of beliefs (the Creed).

The system of ministry was based on the already existing system of elders and deacons. But unlike Paul's opinion, who believed that ministers should be chosen by the gift of the Holy Spirit, they were officially appointed, though it was presumed that they carried the gift within them. This was not a new system of ministry; instead, it had been adapted from the older tradition of elders choosing their successors. The chosen minister was ordained to his office by the imposition of hands (also called the laying on of hands). In the early days, there was no distinction between the clergy and layman; they were all referred to as the royal priests.

The next turning point in the development of the church's organization happened around 96 CE when the Roman Church wrote the First Epistle of Clement. In it, the Christian community of Corinth is addressed, and an attempt is made to solve the schism that was occurring there. A group of elders was disposed of in Corinth, and the Church of Rome urged the community to restore them because they were directly elected successors of the apostles. But another script, the *Didache*, dated to the 1st century CE, reveals that the system of elders was not universal in the early Christian Church. It clearly states that in some communities, prophets and teachers were regarded with high authority. But this document also instructed the church to install bishops and deacons if there were not enough prophets and teachers.

The ministry of bishops has its origins in the Greek secular office of *episkopos*, overseers or supervisors. It came to be a synonym for an elder or presbyter. At first, the bishops were many, and they governed the church together. In time, one man took power in his hands and collected the obligations of various ministries to exercise alone. To distinguish this powerful individual from other presbyters, the term "bishop" came into use. This new system of church organization is called the monarchical episcopate, and it first appeared at the end of the 1ˢᵗ century CE in Antioch, where Bishop Ignatius Theophorus (died anywhere between 108 and 140) resided and worked. While on his way to Rome, where he would become a martyr, Ignatius wrote various letters in which he explained the role of bishops, among other things. In his view, the bishop was central to the congregation, and important functions of the church were in his hands. Ignatius believed that bishops should have the highest authority in the church but that they should always work for the good of the community.

By the mid-2ⁿᵈ century CE, this system was established in the majority of Christian churches. The success of this organization is due to the community's needs for just one main leader, a person who would symbolically represent Jesus at the Eucharist. But this wasn't the end of the obligations a bishop had. He also had to keep communication with other churches alive, represent his church at gatherings, and act as a focal point of communal unity and faith. And not just anyone was eligible to become a bishop. At first, bishops were chosen because they could prove they were direct successors of the original twelve apostles. This guaranteed his ability to keep the oral tradition alive just as his predecessors had taught it.

The second point of the church's reorganization was the issuing of specially selected writings, known as the Scripture. The result was the canon of the New Testament, which contained what the church thought was the authentic tradition and experience of Jesus. The writings were chosen due to their connection with the original apostles and because they preached the orthodox doctrine. But since the accounts of Jesus's life were so different, the church settled on those that had the same essence.

As for their authenticity, the church never questioned it; it believes the writings were authored by the apostles or those close to them. However, some were not satisfied with this dogmatic approach. Writing could not become canonical unless a connection with the apostles was proven. For example, the Epistle to the Hebrews wasn't quoted for nearly two hundred years in the Western churches until it was proven that it was written by someone close to Saint Paul. Scholars still argue over the authorship of this book of the New Testament, but it is now considered canonical.

The Christian canon was complete by the end of the 1st century, but many writings were left out because they had to be confirmed. In the West, the finalization of the canon was achieved between 380 and 390; it was not finalized in the East until later.

The third means of upholding the authority of the church was creating a Creed, the "Rule of Faith." These were the collections of the main teachings of the bishops. The earliest creed can be found in the writings of a Greek bishop named Irenaeus (130-202). He wrote that Christianity is the belief in one God, the creator of everything, who became incarnate in Jesus Christ and in the Holy Spirit, which inspired prophets to forewarn the coming of the end and the path to salvation through Jesus Christ.

The church built its structure on these three doctrines: the bishops who were direct successors of the apostles, the canonical Scripture, and the authoritative Creed. But still, the church had to think about how to link up all the congregations and create a sense of unity. Up until then, it was enough for the different congregations to be aware of their unity in Jesus Christ. But as the church grew, the bishops decided they needed more tangible ways to stay connected. At first, personal visits between churches were an unofficial obligation of the bishops and priests. The religious representatives of one region would gather in synods to discuss common problems. The first such synod we are aware of occurred in Asia, around 170 CE. Over time, some churches took control over the smaller ones in the region. They became metropolitan seats, and they were raised above other churches in the region. Three of them received the status of supra-metropolitan seats in 325 (in the Council of Nicaea): Alexandria, Rome, and Antioch. This status gave them the right to control other churches, mainly the ones with metropolitan statuses.

Rome displayed certain characteristics that eventually raised it above all other churches. Its destiny would be to represent the central power of Christian unity. The Church of Rome achieved such a status because it could historically claim to be the see of Saint Paul and Saint Peter. (A see is a diocese or region that a bishop oversees.) Rome was also the capital of the empire, and as such, the political currents dictated the status of its church. The fact that Rome was also the capital of the empire greatly contributed to the church's wealth. But it wasn't simply Rome's wealth that put it on a high pedestal; it was also willing to share money with other churches and those in need. Famous for its altruism, the Church of Rome was also open to sharing its knowledge, and the visits of other religious representatives of different theological thought were always welcomed.

Chapter 4 – From Persecutions to the Religion of the Emperor

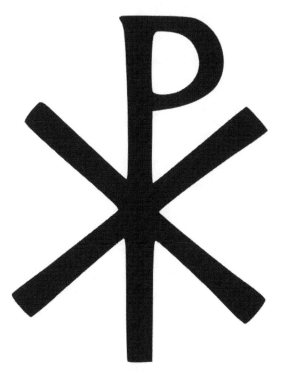

The Chi-Rho Christogram of Constantine, which was painted on the shields of his soldiers.
https://upload.wikimedia.org/wikipedia/commons/7/7b/Simple_Labarum2.svg

The Christian Church didn't face only internal disintegration due to the lack of authority in its early stages. Another threat came from the outside: the Roman state and its government. The empire saw Christianity as a threat to its cultural and political unity, and it started persecuting its followers. But these persecutions, which would last for over two centuries, also helped the spread of Christianity. It became based on the martyrdom of many individuals who lost their lives fighting the oppressive state. But the era of the Christian persecutions didn't simply end with the emperor making peace with the new religion. Instead, it ended with a glorifying victory of the church, as Emperor Constantine the Great sided with the Christians.

In principle, Rome enacted a policy of religious tolerance, which allowed many religions and cults to flourish within the empire. The Christians were treated no differently than other citizens of the empire. But once they started dominating and attracting the masses, the Roman government was worried about the social order, cultural unity, and political domination. Christians suddenly became a threat to the regime. The first persecution of Christians occurred during the reign of Emperor Nero. He exploited public opinion, which claimed Christians were atheists because they didn't want to join the pagan ceremonies and rituals. Nero had the support of the public to eliminate the Christians. However, Nero and his immediate successor never launched an empire-wide persecution of Christians. They were tyrants, and they only cared about the immediate threat closest to them within the walls of Rome.

In the 3rd century, the Roman government finally decided to deal with the threat of Christianity more seriously. The reason was purely religious this time. The Christian Church proclaimed that it was the only true church and that God was the only true deity. The Christians even dared to demand that Romans denounce their pagan gods and rites as false. Moreover, the Christians only obeyed the government and the emperor in matters that were in complete harmony with the will of the one true God. Rome responded by issuing edicts to the provincial governors to relentlessly persecute the Christians.

Septimius Severus (193-211) was the first Roman emperor to issue such an edict. The persecutions of the Christians subsided with the succession of Emperor Severus Alexander (222-235), who put Jesus on a pedestal together with the Roman gods. He even wanted to build a temple dedicated to Christ but was discouraged by the Roman pagan priesthood. When Maximilian took the throne in 235, the persecutions continued with renewed vigor. Peace came again with Emperor Philip the Arab (244-249). Unfortunately, this peace didn't last long, as the next ruler, Emperor Trajan Decius (249-251), intended to strengthen the old Roman pagan religion, and he could only do this by subduing the Christians.

The most severe persecutions of the Christians started during the reign of Emperor Diocletian (284-305). It was inspired by the writings of a philosopher named Porphyry of Tyre, who published his work *Against Christians* in 303. In this text, Porphyry mocked Jesus as being a weak individual, and he mocked Christian altruism. He also attacked the sacred Scripture, pointing out how it was inconsistent and beyond logic.

During the reign of Diocletian, the whole empire was enveloped in a feeling of insecurity. The barbaric hordes tried to attack the empire from all sides, and the empire itself was too large to mount a universal defense. This is why Diocletian implemented a new form of government; he established two co-emperors to supervise the 101 Roman provinces. The empire was not only threatened by barbarian attacks but also by internal division. This was all reflected in the everyday lives of the citizens who were no longer able to safely conduct their business and travel between cities.

The Roman Empire was deeply troubled, and the Christians were apparently to blame because they defied the old Roman gods and represented everything that was against traditional Roman virtue. During one pagan ceremony, Roman priests claimed that it was the presence of Christians that caused his ritual to fail. He stated that the Christians, who occupied many of the governmental offices by this point, were to blame for the danger in which the empire found itself. This was the final straw that convinced Diocletian to persecute the Christians. In February 303, he issued an edict ordering the destruction of all Christian temples and sacred books. Christians were also denied the protection of the law and were forbidden from gathering.

During the next ten years, the church would undergo agony. In another edict, Diocletian singled out the religious leaders of the Christians and arrested them. Later, he even started arresting any suspicious-looking Christians. The religious leaders who were confined were tortured. Their eyes were gouged out, their tongues cut off, and their feet and hands were sawed off. They died either on the stake, acting as food to wild animals during national ceremonies, or in dungeons. During the reigns of the successors of Diocletian, Galerius, and Maximinus Dia, the tortures of the Christians continued, mainly in the East, where they grew in numbers and even represented the majority in some of the cities.

The persecutions of the Christians came to a halt during the second half of the reign of Maximinus, and it is very puzzling why the emperor would suddenly change his mind. But there was a reasonable explanation for it. This series of events concerning the succession of the divided empire brought forth a very powerful conqueror: Constantine. Ruling over Italy and Africa, Constantine became the sole ruler of the known Western world, and he was powerful enough to put pressure on Maximinus regarding Christians. Constantine attributed his good luck in the conquest of the Western world, which he achieved by 312, to the Christian God. He even claimed he had a vision of Jesus Christ, who ordered him to put Christian symbols on the shields of his soldiers to secure victory.

Constantine the Great and Christianity

Obeying the vision of Christ, Constantine rendered all the shields to be decorated with the Christogram *chi-rho*, which was the beginning letters of Christ's name in Greek (ΧΡΙΣΤΟΣ). The young emperor did win the battle against his enemies, but he didn't convert to Christianity. Although he believed in monotheism from a young age, and he certainly was moved by some kind of religious experience, he couldn't convert due to political pressure. His vast empire was still pagan, and he understood it would take time for the people to completely convert. Until that happened, he could not risk the anger of his followers by converting to a minority religion.

Nevertheless, during the next decade, Constantine showed his affection for Christianity. In 313, he met with Maximinus, who ruled the eastern part of the empire, and pressured him into agreeing on complete religious tolerance. Christians were to be free and even allowed to retrieve all of their property and preach their religion as they saw fit. Gradually, Constantine started suppressing paganism. In his early days, he still acted as the supreme pontiff of the pagan religion, and he paid homage to the sun god. But later, he started publicly displaying Christian symbols and imposing various restrictions on pagan ceremonies and rituals. Constantine's true acceptance of Christians would only come once he started identifying the state's interests as being the same as the church's interests. He hoped to achieve the unity of the state and the church, and he would use his imperial power to meddle in religious affairs.

In 324, Constantine became the sole ruler of the entire empire. Immediately, he had to deal with the dispute that arose within the church, which threatened its unity as well as the unity of the empire. It happened in Alexandria. A presbyter dared to challenge his bishop on the matter of Jesus and God and their relation as Son and the Father. Constantine tried to urge the church to ignore such small inconsistencies in the doctrine, but the matter only escalated. Finally, in May of 325, the emperor gathered more than two hundred of the empire's bishops in the first general ecumenical council known as the First Council of Nicaea. The emperor took a personal interest in the debate and even joined the council on a few occasions. But it seemed that the matter wouldn't be easily settled, and it continued to bring disunity in the church until the death of Constantine in 337.

Constantine showed his appreciation of Christianity by lavishing the church with many gifts. He also ordered the construction of many beautiful basilicas throughout the empire. The most famous ones would be in Rome on the supposed site of the tomb of Saint Peter and in Jerusalem, where Christ's tomb lies. Constantine even gifted his palace in Rome (the Lateran Palace) to the bishop, and it remained the main papal residence until 1308. In 324, the emperor moved the capital of the empire to Byzantium, which was then renamed Constantinople. There, he erected numerous Christian churches, among which two were of significant beauty; one was dedicated to peace, and the other one to the apostles.

To support Christianity, Constantine modified the Roman law so it could conform to Christian moral values. He also elevated the Christian clergy as a new social class, freeing them of forced labor obligations and military service. He also vested the civil authority into bishops so they could deal with the judicial decisions within the church. He officially declared Sunday to be the day of rest because it was the day when Christians assembled. Constantine set the path for the unification of the church and the state, and he is thus regarded as the architect of the Middle Ages.

Under Constantine, the state and the church were in an alliance. They were not yet considered one as they would be in the centuries to come, but they still worked together for the good of the empire. But this alliance had some drawbacks that would influence the church's future development. People decided to convert not because they saw the truth in Christ but because it would bring social conformity to Constantine's empire. The bishops started exploiting their civil authority to achieve their political aspirations. The church went from being persecuted to persecuting the nonconformists.

Constantine truly changed the church, for better and for worse. Although he was only baptized on his deathbed, he had indeed been converted since his early days of conquest (the official date of his conversion is regarded to be 312 by the church). Thus, he represents not only one of the greatest points of the history of the church but also of the world.

Christian Victory Over Paganism

Constantine the Great never made Christianity the official religion of the empire because Christians were still a minority. And they remained so during the whole 4th century. But at its end, the tides turned, and the Christians grew so greatly that Emperor Theodosius made it an official religion in 380. What changed in the years after Constantine to bring such an influx of people to the church? Christianity was a prominent religion in urban centers, and it appealed mostly to the middle and lower urban classes. But after its recognition in the eyes of the emperor, the faith started spreading outside of the cities and into the countryside. Peasants started joining the church in great numbers, and the missionaries started freely traveling through the countryside. Up until the conversion of Constantine, the peasants were stubborn in worshiping their ancestral deities. There was also the problem of language, as many villages remained true to their Thracian, Berber, Coptic, or Celtic tongues. But these barriers were knocked down once the official approval of the faith came, as many missionaries who spoke different languages embarked on a quest of conversion.

Another group of citizens that was very stubborn in remaining pagan was the aristocrats. Due to their upbringing and education, they couldn't simply let go of their old deities and moral values. But a time came when their old religion would prevent them from socially advancing. Suddenly, the Christians had all the social and political privileges, as most of the senators were Christians, and the aristocrats finally agreed to convert.

This social movement started much earlier during the reign of Diocletian, as he made it possible for the lower classes to assume official positions in the government. This helped spread Christianity further because there were no stubborn aristocrats in high offices to pose a threat to the new religious thought. Constantine expanded the size of the Senate and brought thousands of new members who had their origin in the middle class. Many of them were already Christians, while others were willing to convert to the religion. Thus, Constantine ignored the old aristocracy and made his own Christian one.

By the 4th century, there was no pagan political resistance in the eastern part of the empire. But in the West, the situation was significantly different. In Rome, the Senate remained largely pagan, and they refused to obey Constantine's order to remove the images of their old gods from the Senate chambers. But Constantine's three sons, his successors, assumed a harder stance, especially Constantius II, who started his sole rule of the empire in 353. He was resolute on exterminating paganism, and he ordered the closure of all the temples and a death sentence for anyone who participated in sacrificial ceremonies to the old gods. The pagans continued their worship in major centers such as Rome, Alexandria, and Heliopolis, but they were in a very difficult position.

Christianity started dominating during the reign of Constantius, but this dominance was challenged with his successor, Emperor Julian, who assumed the throne in 361 and proclaimed himself pagan. Julian grew up in the imperial home and was baptized as Christian. However, he associated the faith with the bloodbath that followed Constantine's death in 337. Julian was the son of Constantine's half-brother, who was killed by his nephews to prevent a succession dispute. Julian was spared, as he was just a little boy at the time, but he remembered the death of his father, and in his boyish mind, he made a connection between his father's assassination and Christianity. Even though he was officially Christian, he read pagan books and secretly worshiped pagan gods. Once he assumed power, he abandoned his Christian mask and showed his true face. In the history of Christianity, he is remembered as Julian the Apostate.

As soon as he succeeded the throne, Julian started revising all of the religious policies of his Christian predecessors, and he went to great lengths to restore the old Roman religion, which he saw as the pinnacle of cultural and spiritual life. The priests lost the privileges that they were granted under Constantine and Constantius. The display of Christian symbols was prohibited, and they were replaced with the old pagan symbols. The emperor ordered the reinstallment of the sacrificial rites and the invocation of all the old gods, such as Jupiter, Mars, Apollo, Bacchus, and Venus.

But Julian's reorganization of the state religion didn't appeal to the masses. They regarded paganism as old, as ideas and philosophies that had no relevance in modern times. Christianity was still very much attractive because it had a simple but vital message of love. Christianity brought renewed morality, and it freed the people from the senseless repetition of ceremonies and rites.

Emperor Julian had a very brief reign. He was killed by the Persians on the sands of far-away Mesopotamia in 363. His death marked the end of paganism and the victory of Christianity throughout the Roman Empire.

This became clear when Julian's soldiers elected Jovian, a general who was known for his Christian faith, as the next emperor. As soon as he came to power, he reinstalled Christianity as the official religion of the empire and returned the status and privileges to the clergy and the church. He ruled for only one year, but the next emperor the army chose, Valentinian I, was also Christian. Valentinian shared the rule with his brother Valens because he needed a trustworthy co-ruler to defend the empire from attacks from the Franks, Saxons, and Goths. However, Valens failed his defense of the Danube border and was killed in 378. His death started the downfall of the empire. But while the empire was crumbling, the church continued to grow, not only in numbers but also in power.

The Roman state transformed into a totalitarian regime, and the civic and political freedoms of the people disappeared. In these times of great need, the church was the bastion of freedom. In it, the people continued to have a sense of greater purpose and of belonging to a community. The people felt as if they could control at least part of their destiny, a spiritual part.

Aside from religious liberty, the church offered material assistance to those who needed it. And with the new regime, many people felt the economic strains pressing upon them. The church had a magnificent system of charity that continued to appeal to the masses, especially in times of great stress. This system included various institutions such as orphanages, homes for the old and aged, hospitals, and even inns for travelers. Due to the constant barbarian attacks, the state soon became unable to cope with the social distress, and it started heavily relying on the church.

At this point, the bishops received judicial power over the matters of social welfare. But as spiritual leaders, the bishops had to lead by example, and that often meant eating and sleeping with the poor and renouncing all worldly possessions. The prestige and influence of the bishops grew, and soon they started enjoying immense popularity. Emperors Gratian (r. 367–383) and Theodosius I (r. 379–395) recognized the immense influence the church had on the people, and they turned it into a foundation on which the whole social order should stand. They not only confirmed Christianity as the official religion of the empire, but they also made paganism illegal.

Furthermore, the Christian religious leaders acquired even more privileges, such as exemption from secular trials and the establishment of the ecclesiastical courts. Roman law, which already followed Christian values, was expanded even more to encompass Christian principles. The old pagan calendar was revised to meet Christian needs, and Christmas and Easter were made official state holidays. The pagan priesthood was completely abolished, and many old activities were proclaimed heresy. In 382, the old statue of Victory was finally removed from the public Senate building in Rome, although many pagans protested it.

The authority of the church is probably best seen in the episode in which Emperor Theodosius I ordered the massacre of civilians in Thessaloniki, as he was angered by the assassination of a chariot racer. The church took the side of the people and ordered Theodosius to commit a public penance for the massacre. Until Christmas, the emperor visited church each day without his royal garments as a commoner. On Christmas Day, Bishop Ambrose of Milan finally accepted the emperor's penance and admitted him back to communion.

Chapter 5 – Monasticism

Saint Jerome with Saint Paula and Saint Eustochium by Francisco de Zurbarán, 17th century. Now in the National Gallery of Art, Washington.

https://en.wikipedia.org/wiki/Paula_of_Rome#/media/File:Francisco_de_Zurbar%C3%A1n_043.jpg

The first Christian monasteries were first established at the beginning of the 4ᵗʰ century. The first monasteries were founded in Egypt, and they spread through both the Eastern and Western Christian worlds. Monasteries and monks were not the inventions of the church. In fact, they existed in many other religions throughout the world; some scholars believe that pagan monasticism penetrated Christianity and produced the first Christian monasteries. The monastic life certainly shaped the history of Christianity from the 4ᵗʰ century until the Reformation in 1517. Even today, the monasteries of both Catholic and Orthodox Christianity play an important role in the lives of believers.

The first traces of what resembled monastic life in Christianity can be traced back as far as 250 CE, when some of the Jewish Christians practiced what was known as asceticism. They vowed celibacy and fasting for life. Other Christian communities started accepting the ascetic way of life to which they added the practice of philosophy. During the early Roman persecutions of Christians, these ascetics ran to the wilderness for personal safety. There, they lived as hermits, trying to reach perfection. However, most of the early ascetics lived close to their congregations, sometimes even in their centers. They had families and were productive members of society but continued to practice fasting and celibacy. When Christianity became the religion of the masses during Emperor Constantine's reign, these ascetics no longer felt at home in the big cities of, for example, Constantinople, Rome, and Alexandria. They decided to retreat to deserted places like mountains, forests, and deserts, where they would pray for their salvation in peace, away from the urban life.

This means that monastic life started as a protest against the alliance between the state and the church. The ascetics wanted to preserve the purity of the church by transplanting it away from the masses, from cities into the wilderness. They thought that the church had turned to pagan moral corruption and only resembled

Christianity in its appearance. It was the holy duty of these individuals to preserve the virginity of their faith. Another problem the ascetics saw in the union of the state and the church was the disappearance of martyrdom. For them, monastic life was the compensation for the lack of newly sanctified martyrs. Thus, the early ascetics who moved into the caves of the Egyptian and Syrian deserts started self-torture and restricted themselves from any worldly pleasures to gain entrance to the Kingdom of Heaven. Previous martyrs would gain access to this kingdom through their sacrifice to the faith. But with the union of the state and the church, there was no more fighting against the regime and no more persecutions to endure.

The Development of Monasticism

There were four distinctive stages of the development of monastic life. It could be said that the first three stages occurred during the 4th century, and the last one began with the Latin Church of the Middle Ages. The first stage was when asceticism started within the church. The people vowed to engage in celibacy and fasting but continued their daily urban lives together with the rest of Christian society. The clergymen who dedicated themselves to the ascetic way of life were not yet monks, as they continued to operate in the church. The second stage was when the ascetics decided to remove themselves from society and start living as hermits. The prophets Elijah and John the Baptist served as role models of this anchorite model, but 4th-century hermits took it to even greater extremes with complete seclusion. These individuals, which included Paul of Thebes and Saint Anthony, decided to cut off any contact with society, except for special occasions when they received visitors who came to admire them or seek spiritual guidance from them. They lived alone in the wilderness and had no possessions. A cave was their home, and their hair their garment. They ate bread and salt and devoted their lives to prayer and fantastical battles with demons. Hermeticism developed in the East, but it proved too extreme for Western believers. The climate was much rougher there, which made complete seclusion impossible. Hermits still existed, but they were much less frequent than in the East.

The third stage of monastic life is coenobitism, which was when people who practiced asceticism decided to group together. This is the beginning of the monasticism we know today. The first to start monastic lives were the Therapeutae and Essenes, which were Jewish religious sects. Modern scholars believe that Saint Pachomius (also known as Pachomius the Great) followed their example when he started the first monastery in Egypt. Pachomius was born in Thebes to pagan parents, but once he was recruited into the Roman army, he encountered Christianity. When he learned about the ascetics, he wanted to pursue that way of life. But it wasn't until he chose the path of hermetic solitude that a vision came to him to build a place where hermits could gather.

Saint Pachomius started his first monastery sometime between 318 and 323 in Tabennisi, Egypt. Many hermits joined him, and soon the monastery grew to house over one hundred men. But these hermits wanted to devote their lives to prayer, and Saint Pachomius took it upon himself to organize the monastery and administer it alone. Because of this, the hermits named him "Father," which is "Abba" in Hebrew, hence the modern word abbot. For the most part, the monks shared responsibilities and divided their time between prayers and daily labor. In time, they started relying on their production more than on the goodwill of the people outside the monastery. Rather than living from alms, the monks started collecting them for the poor. This type of secluded yet communal existence was attractive to both sexes, and male and female monasteries started developing.

The development of the monasteries didn't lead to the end of the hermetic way of life. In fact, many monks decided to continue or start living as hermits. Nevertheless, the number of hermits dropped. With the increase in the number of monks, some kind of organization was needed, and soon monasteries started grouping together under one government. This is how the monastic orders came to be, especially with the spread of monasticism in the East by Saint Pachomius and in the West by Saint Benedict.

Saint Jerome

Of all the church fathers of the 4th century, Jerome of Stridon was the most zealous supporter and promoter of monastic life. But he was more than that; he was also the link that connected the teachings of the Eastern and Western Churches. Because of this, the life of Saint Jerome is a historical tale of both the church and monasticism. He was the first among the learned church individuals who embraced the monastic life and made monasteries the centers of learning, as well as of religious devotion. He promoted ascetic piety, but he was also a very talented man with an active mind. He translated and interpreted the Bible, proving that passion and ambition can be united with spirituality and faith.

Saint Jerome's given name was Eusebius Sophronius Hieronymus. He was born between 340 and 347 in a place known as Stridon. We don't know exactly where Stridon was, but we know it was either in today's Croatia, or Slovenia, which were once part of the Roman province of Dalmatia. Jerome's parents were wealthy Christians, and he was given a good education in the city of Rome. Some of his most prominent teachers were pagan, such as the grammarian Donatus, but Saint Jerome remained true to his Christian heritage. In his school days, he developed a love for poetry, rhetoric, and philosophy, and through his life, he collected a considerable library. In around 370, Saint Jerome was baptized in Rome, and he went to Gaul and Trier to continue his theological studies. But during his later travels through Antioch, he became severely ill and had a vision of Christ, who persuaded him to fully devote himself to the study of the Bible. Saint Jerome renounced secular studies and abandoned reading the famous classics, vowing he would never touch worldly books again.

Later in life, Saint Jerome didn't strictly keep to his oath. He found that his knowledge of secular teachings would greatly help him linguistically shape his interpretation of the Bible. He learned how to bind his classical knowledge in the service of God and religion. To inspire other monks, he made them copy Cicero's dialogues. He often cited ancient authors such as Virgil in his later writings. So, the life of Jerome became one divided between the asceticism of the East and the literary works of the West. He chose to benefit from both worlds, and he combined Eastern discipline with his Western mindset and thirst for knowledge.

While in Antioch and the Syrian Desert, Saint Jerome devoted himself to asceticism. He spent some time living as a hermit, and he claims that it was then that he came to realize Christ and his love for humanity. From this point, Saint Jerome would always strive to live ascetically. Although he was torn between the East and the West, between being a hermit and a learned individual, he would find a compromise in monasticism.

Jerome was ordained by Bishop Paulinus in Antioch, but he never took charge of a congregation. Instead, in 380, he went to Constantinople, where he started his translation work. First, he translated the *Chronicle* of Eusebius and the homilies of Origen on Jeremiah and Ezekiel. In 382, Jerome returned to Rome with Bishop Paulinus, who introduced him to Bishop Damasus. It was Damasus who employed Jerome to revise the Latin version of the Bible.

While in Rome, Jerome devoted his time to promoting monasticism, both by writing about it and by giving speeches. Monastic life had gained a small foothold in the West, and despite Jerome's efforts, it encountered a string of opposition in the clergy. Jerome hoped his promotion of monastic life would appeal to the rich families of Rome, the descendants of the Scipios, Marcelluses, and others who would then turn their villas into monasteries. He urged the wealthiest among them to turn toward a life of charity and self-sacrifice. The spiritually starved population of Rome listened to Jerome, and his propaganda of monastic life had great success.

Wealthy women were especially attracted to monastic life. They were either the widows of aristocrats, such as Marcella, Albina, and the most admired Paula, or they were virgins, such as Marcellina, Apella, and Demetrias. Saint Jerome found that the aristocratic ladies of Rome were already well-read in the Holy Scripture and eager to listen to his ideas. After listening to Jerome's teachings of monastic life, these ladies of Rome vowed celibacy and devoted their lives to prayer and the study of the Scripture. They were not yet nuns, which already existed in the East, but they led solitary lives that would later be known as the convent life.

Jerome was certain that asceticism was the true and perfect form of Christianity, but he missed the companionship of others, and it was in these women that he would find devoted friends. Jerome preached the importance of virginity and the evilness of a second marriage to them. He even went as far as to diminish the meaning of marriage, viewing it as a poor reward for weak-minded men who could not stand to have an empty bed. According to him, Mary, Mother of God, was a virgin when she gave birth to Jesus, and she remained a virgin even though she continued her life as a wife of Joseph. It was Jerome who introduced the doctrine of the perpetual virginity of the Mother of God into Catholic Christianity.

In 384, Jerome left Rome again and took Paula and her daughter Eustochium on a pilgrimage to Jerusalem. There, the trio made their permanent residence, claiming they would devote their lives to lamenting their past sins. Jerome founded a monastery in Bethlehem, where he remained until the end of his days. The organization of the monastery was influenced by the Egyptian ones, but it was adapted to the Latin mindset. The monks lived in separate cells where they prayed, but they took their meals together. They also labored together to support themselves and had communal prayers at different intervals throughout the day. Jerome also built a hospital and devoted the remainder of his life to his literary work. He finally took time to finish revising the Latin version of the Bible, which became his most important work, a monument to his life. His fame attracted many monks to Bethlehem, but Jerome constantly complained about how crowded his monastery became. Saint Jerome died of fever in 420; he was between seventy-three and seventy-eight years old when he died.

Saint Paula

Saint Paula was Jerome's most distinguished disciple, and she became the model of the Roman Catholic nun. She was a descendant of the Scipio and Gracchi aristocratic and senatorial families of Rome, and she was born in 347. Everything we know of Paula's life comes from the letters of Saint Jerome. He described her as a great Roman lady who dressed in silk and was carried around by her servants. She was married to a nobleman but became a widow when she was thirty-two years old. She was the mother of five children, and she remained devoted to her family after her husband's death but turned more and more to the religious texts. Paula was influenced by the life of Saint Marcella, a female ascetic, and she dedicated her own life to similar values even before she met Saint Jerome. Once they met in 382, they quickly became friends. Paula renounced her worldly wealth and pleasures and adopted a rigorously ascetic life.

Paula joined Jerome in the pilgrimage to Jerusalem, passing through Palestine and Egypt. On her travels, she learned of the monastic ways of the Egyptian ascetics, and once in Bethlehem, she opened a separate monastery for women, though it was physically joined with the monastery founded by Jerome. Men and women had separate cells, and they ate and worked completely separately. However, they had joint prayers during the day. The female monastery was divided into three different sections, each housing women depending on their social status. Saint Paula first used her family wealth to finance the construction of the monastery, but when it was done, she opened an inn for travelers, which would continue to provide the covenant with money. She also spent her family wealth by giving alms to the poor, and she continued living in poverty.

Saint Jerome often wrote of Paula's intellectual abilities, chastity, and perpetual fasting. She denied herself and her daughter Eustochium food and wine. She slept on the ground, or she would spend the whole night praying, even when she was ill. She felt guilty about her previous life and wanted to disfigure her face because she used to wear makeup. She also wanted to punish her body, as she used it to make love to her husband, and she wanted to constantly weep to make up for the laughter of her previous life. Paula's greatest wish was to die as a beggar and to be buried in a shroud that wasn't her possession. When she did die in 404, she left her daughter in great debt, as she had taken the family wealth to finance her monastery and the alms for the poor.

Saint Benedict

Saint Benedict of Nursia fixed monasticism in the Western world and gave it a permanent form. The order bears his name because he is regarded as the patriarch of the Western monks. He elevated the Eastern tradition into a much more organized form and gave it a practical and literary character. Although Benedict was born in 480, more than half a century after Saint Jerome had passed, he displayed a similar zealousness about asceticism and the monastic form of life.

He was born in Nursia, Umbria, in modern-day Italy. At this time, Europe was in a state of distress due to constant conflicts between the pagans and the developing Christian kingdoms. Benedict studied in Rome but was quickly repulsed by the immoral and corrupt behavior of his fellow students. He sought seclusion and found it in Subiaco in a sacred grotto. There, he had a neighboring monk who supplied him with food by sending it down in the grotto with a rope.

In this dark and inaccessible grotto, Saint Bernard fought his anchoritic battle with his inner demons. Pope Gregory I was the first to write about the life of Saint Benedict, but he wrote it sometime after 593, a long time after Benedict's death. The writings of Pope Gregory are filled with imagined episodes. Even the authenticity of his work is often disputed by Catholic scholars. In one of the episodes, the pope wrote how Saint Benedict was consumed by lust to the point where he was ready to go after a woman. But he had a strong will and resisted. To make his body suffer, Benedict rolled around in thorns and briers, which eventually extinguished his worldly desires. Benedict devoted himself to the ascetic life so much that the local shepherds who saw him on a few occasions thought he was a wild beast.

After the period he spent living as a hermit, Saint Benedict joined a proper monastery and started his labors in communal life. He established twelve cloisters in the mountainous region of Subiaco, each having twelve monks and one superior. He was the overseer of all twelve monastic cloisters. Around 530, Benedict left Subiaco. The legend tells of a priest named Florentius, who was jealous of Benedict and his success in attracting monks who wanted to study under him. Florentius tried to poison the saint, but he failed. Then he tried to tempt his disciples with local prostitutes but failed in that as well. Finally, Benedict decided to leave only to avoid the wrath of Florentius and his malicious temptations.

Saint Benedict chose to settle in the mountains of the Neapolitan province, where he dedicated himself to the destruction of idols and the conversion of the pagan settlers. He performed miracles and preached, and he founded the cloister of Monte Cassino upon the ruins of an old sanctuary dedicated to the pagan god Apollo. This would become the alma mater and the capital of the Benedictine order. Saint Benedict was never ordained into the priesthood, and his life in Monte Cassino was one of a missionary. He abandoned the solitary life and started preaching to the young monks.

Together, they cultivated the land so they could feed the poor and heal the sick. He was loved by the people to whom he preached, and even a pagan king of Italy, Totila, who visited him in 542, fell on his knees before the holiness of Saint Benedict. King Totila converted to Christianity but died ten years later, just as Benedict had predicted. In 547, Saint Benedict died in prayer while standing in front of the altar of his monastery.

The life of Saint Benedict might not have been as interesting as those of Saint Bernard of Clairvaux (founder of the Cistercian order) or Saint Francis of Assisi (founder of the Franciscan order), but he was the founder of monasticism in the West. Benedict's fame lies in the *Rule of Saint Benedict* (Latin: *Regula Sancti Benedicti*), a book of instructions for monks who lived in a monastery, which he wrote in 516. In a very short time, the *Regula Sancti Benedicti* surpassed other similar rules that already existed and became the basis of Catholic monastic life. It has a preface and seventy-two chapters in which Saint Benedict describes moral, liturgical, penal, and even social ordinances. This book made the strict Eastern monastic life appeal to the Western mindset by uniting discipline and gentleness and simplicity with completeness.

Chapter 6 – Papal Primacy

Pope Leo III crowning Charlemagne, painted by Friedrich Kaulbach in 1861.
*https://en.wikipedia.org/wiki/Charlemagne#/media/File:Kaulbach_Die_Kaiserkr%C3%B6
nung_Karls_des_Gro%C3%9Fen.jpg*

During the 4th and 5th centuries, the papacy tried to impose its superiority over the whole Christian Church. Before this, the church didn't need a superior overseer or the jurisdiction of the pope or any other religious leader. But the social changes of Early Medieval Europe demanded a new type of leadership. The bishops started acting as shepherds to the ecumenical society, and even the whispers of an ecumenical state started developing. The first bishop of Rome who officially demanded the supremacy of the papacy over all churches was Pope Damasus I (papacy 366–384). At the ecumenical council of 382, he explained that this primacy was bestowed by the Lord himself on Saint Peter, who was the first bishop of Rome; in other words, Peter was the first pope. The first pope who started taking the initiative on the matter was Pope Siricius (papacy 384–399). In his decretals (decisions on ecclesiastical law), Siricius claimed the right to make decisions on both doctrinal and disciplinary matters alone.

The claims Pope Siricius asserted received mixed feelings in the West and strong opposition in the East. But the strongest opposition at the time came from the African church, which wanted to remain independent. However, it was Pope Leo I (papacy 440–461) who represented the turning point of the papacy's history. Pope Leo was a great statesman who put himself in the service of the church, and for his work, he earned the surname "the Great." Leo had a very commanding character and was a diplomatic genius who drew on previous papal experiences and claims to formulate a doctrine of papal supremacy. He explained that Saint Peter was the "rock" on which the church was built, just like Jesus said it would be. The bishops of Rome were not only the successors of Saint Peter but also personified him. Thus, the office of the pope (the bishop of Rome) meant that he was the supreme ruler of the universal church. Other bishops were there only to help the pope and share some of his responsibilities.

Pope Leo I didn't only express his wish for papal superiority, but he also claimed authority in Spain and Africa. Valentinian III, Western Emperor of the Roman Empire, issued an edict in 445, which proclaimed that the primacy of the apostolic see in Rome must be observed. This edict wouldn't see the light of day without the scheming of Leo. The same Emperor Valentinian was assassinated in 455, and Pope Leo I jumped to fill the vacuum of secular rule that ensued in the city of Rome. But even before that, Leo showed his impressive care for the city's well-being by meeting with Atilla the Hun in 452 and persuading the pagan leader to abandon his plans of sacking the city. Several years later, in 455, another barbarian leader, Gaiseric the Vandal, attacked Rome. Pope Leo failed to persuade him to refrain from attacking, but he did meet Gaiseric at the gates of the city and urged him to order his men not to destroy anything. The barbarian party sacked the city but spared its beautiful buildings and people.

During the papacy of Pope Leo I, the church experienced one of its most important crises. Leo I took the opportunity to display his authority by imposing himself at the ecumenical council that gathered in 451 in Chalcedon. More than five hundred bishops gathered to discuss the nature of Jesus. Was he human or divine? And could it be that simple to divide in the first place?

It all started much earlier with a monk named Eutyches, who preached the human nature of Jesus Christ. He was found guilty of heresy. The patriarch of Constantinople, Flavian, relieved him of his office, and this would have been the end of the matter if the patriarch of Alexandria, Dioscorus, didn't want to destroy Flavian, whom he saw as his rival. Patriarch Flavian found himself accused of heresy, and he had no other choice but to call a council (Council of Ephesus, 431) to settle the matter.

The Eastern Roman Empire had two major theological schools— one in Alexandria and another in Antioch. At this point, Antioch was determined to defend the stance that Christ was human in nature, and its clergy wouldn't budge. The result was a complete separation of the Oriental Orthodox Church, but not before a great controversy and violence could be averted. In 449, the bishops were threatened by soldiers to sign Flavian's dismissal, who met his death only four days later.

But while all of this was happening at the Council of Ephesus, Pope Leo I was busy writing his masterful piece of dogmatic theological letter, simply named the Tome. In this letter, Leo tried to resolve the issue, and he managed to persuade Pulcheria, sister of Emperor Theodosius II, in the righteousness of his cause. She persuaded her husband and successor to the throne, Marcian, to call for another ecumenical council. By that time, Leo's Tome was already circulating the church, and it was widely accepted and applauded.

At the Council of Chalcedon, of all the bishops gathered, only two were papal legates, and they represented the Western Church. Patriarch Dioscorus was the accused, and his trial lasted until deep into the night. Once the evidence was brought up of his use of force in Ephesus to make the bishops sign Flavian's sentencing, Dioscorus was left without any supporters. The papal legates sentenced him to deposition, invoking the will of Pope Leo I. Other bishops gave their support to the pope, not only in the matter of Dioscorus but also in how he resolved the matter of Christ's dual nature in his Tome. Although the bishops finally agreed on how they should proceed with the orthodox doctrine of the human nature of Christ, the emperor wasn't satisfied. He wanted to ensure the unity of the Eastern and Western churches, and he gathered a committee that would define the doctrine in precise words so it couldn't be brought up again.

The committee quickly presented the first definition of the nature of Christ, and the majority of the bishops were pleased. However, the papal legates were not. They wanted the official definition to use the pope's exact wording of "two natures" instead of the one the committee came up with, which said "of two natures." The committee had to go back and create a definition in accordance with Leo's Tome; otherwise, they could be accused of following the teachings of Dioscorus, who was sentenced for heresy. They didn't want the same fate to fall upon them. The new formulation of the phrase pleased not only the papal legates but also the whole assembly: "One and the same Christ, Son, Lord, Only-begotten, made known in two natures [which exist] without confusion, without change, without division, without separation; the difference of the natures having been in no wise taken away by reason of the union, but rather the properties of each being preserved, and [both] concurring into one Person (prosopon) and one hypostasis—not parted or divided into two Persons (prosopa) but one and the same Son and Only-begotten, the divine Logos, the Lord Jesus Christ."[1]

Pope Leo I might have won this dogmatic battle, but he failed to unite Christendom. The Nestorians of the Eastern Church rejected the formulation of the Council of Chalcedon, mainly because they didn't see how it could fit in the already dogmatic definition of the Holy Trinity. In addition to this schism, Constantinople was now regarded as a rival to Rome. In Canon 28 of the Council of Chalcedon, Constantinople is referred to as "New Rome," and it is explicitly said that the Church of Constantinople was being given the same privileges as the Church of Rome.

Pope Leo was powerless to do anything about the elevation of Constantinople as a metropolitan seat, but he objected and refused to accept the canon. The pope believed that Constantinople would gain the emperor's undivided attention, which would eventually lead to it becoming holier than Rome itself. This would only further degrade the unity of the church. Rome's primacy would be denied only for political reasons because, unlike Rome, Constantinople was not the apostolic seat. Leo not only refused to recognize the elevated position of Constantinople, but he also claimed that Alexandria was the only see with the right to take second place after Rome, as it was founded by Saint Mark.

---

[1] R. V. Sellers, *The Council of Chalcedon*, p. 211. London: S.P.C.K., 1961.

Finally, the patriarch of Constantinople sent a letter to Pope Leo, promising he would not officially promulgate Canon 28. The pope accepted this compromise, and the matter of the two churches was patched up for the time being. However, the matter would continue to bother the two churches and finally lead to a break-up known as the Great Schism. Although Leo I didn't bring about papal primacy, he left the office with a clear sense of the prerogatives that belonged to the apostolic church. This meant that when the empire finally and completely collapsed, the papacy was strong enough to embark on a new mission: the Christianization of the barbarians.

The Path to a United Christendom

When the Roman Empire faced its gradual downfall, the popes didn't despair. First, the imperial administration of the Western Roman Empire collapsed, and the disintegration of Roman society followed. The papal office was well aware of the social changes that were occurring, as the once civilized Romans were now replaced with the invading barbarians. Instead of yearning for the golden age of Rome, the popes turned to the future. The barbarians were there to stay, so it was upon the church to make them Christians and integrate them into the Western image of Christian society. The end of the Western Roman Empire came in 476, and with it, the vision of the papacy's mission took its final shape. Out of the ruins of the Western Roman Empire, they were to shape a new Western society: Christendom.

But the papal office wasn't the only one tirelessly working on the creation of this new society. The patient and slow labor of anonymous monks contributed greatly, and so did the political aspirations of the new Frankish leaders. The process of making a new society was very long; the Western Roman Empire collapsed at the end of the 5th century, and it wouldn't be complete until Charlemagne (r. 800–814) took the crown from the hands of Pope Leo III in the year 800.

The Western Roman Empire didn't fall all at once. Even though we put a concrete date on when it happened, it was more of a gradual collapse caused by the constant pressure on the empire by various Germanic tribes. Over the centuries, these tribes pushed the borders of the empire, with Goths pushing on the Rhine, the Alemanni on the Danube border in southern Germany, the Vandals in Silesia, and the Visigoths in Ukraine and southern Russia. The Germanic tribes exhausted the empire's finances by forcing it to continuously invest in new defenses. Finally, when the Huns appeared in 375, the Ostrogoths managed to penetrate the empire. Fleeing the new raiders from the Eurasian Steppe, they sought refuge within the borders of the Roman Empire, and the emperors had no other choice but to allow them to settle. Hostility between the Romans and the Ostrogoths was evident from the beginning, and it resulted in an open war in 378, in which Emperor Valens lost his life. Weakened, the Roman Empire was unable to defend itself from the barbarians outside of their borders, and in 406, the Vandals settled beyond the Rhine. In 410, the king of the Visigoths, Alaric I, sacked the city of Rome. By 484, the Vandals were ruling North Africa, while the Franks and Alemanni occupied the western shores of the Rhine. Northern and central Gaul was ruled by the descendants of Alaric I of the Visigoths. So, not only the Western Roman Empire but most of Europe were a patchwork of various Germanic kingdoms.

At the time, the Goths and Vandals had already converted, but they belonged to Arianism, a doctrine originating from Alexandria that believes Jesus was the son of God. He was a distinct individual and subordinate to God. The Arian doctrine was and still is considered heresy among most of the mainstream branches of Christianity. With these Germanic tribes taking over the secular power, the Catholic Church found itself in a very poor position. The Arians persecuted Catholics in 484, and the Vandal ruler of Africa officially prohibited assemblies of Christians. He also confiscated all their churches and exiled the bishops from their sees. The Visigoths in Spain were not much better, as they restricted the workings of the Catholic Church.

But when Clovis I (r. 509–511), the ruler of the Franks, came to power, he united the Frankish tribes under one kingdom. Then, he led his Franks against the Gauls north of the Loire and took their territory. Clovis was a pagan, not an Arian, but that was more acceptable to the Catholic Church. He ended up marrying a Catholic princess, and under her influence, he finally converted in 496. His baptism is one of the most important events in Catholic history because he was the founder of the Merovingian dynasty and established the Catholic Frankish Kingdom. Thus, when Charlemagne came to the throne centuries later, the kingdom was already Christian, Catholic, and ready to transform into the Carolingian Empire. This empire would embrace and change Christianity during the medieval period.

But in other parts of western Europe and what once was the Roman Empire, Arian Goths continued persecuting the Catholics. The final catastrophe came in 568 when the Lombards, another Germanic tribe, crossed the Alps and conquered Milan. The Catholic archbishop who had his residence in the city was forced to flee. In 572, the Lombards sacked Rome, which proved to be the final blow to Roman civilization.

In that bleak reality of Early Medieval Europe, one man stood as a shining light of hope, and he occupied the throne of Saint Peter. This man was Pope Gregory the Great. Profoundly spiritual, well-educated, and brilliant, Pope Gregory gave the papacy direction. Gregory was a well-loved individual in Rome because he was a wealthy nobleman who spent all of his riches on founding monasteries and helping the poor. He turned his palace into a monastery, where he continued to live the ascetic life. He was pushed into the papacy because the people had elected him.

Gregory I laid the foundation for the Christendom of the Middle Ages due to four amazing achievements: establishing popes as the de facto rulers of central Italy, strengthening the papal primacy over the Western churches, starting the conversion of the Anglo-Saxons, and shaping medieval Christian thought through his many theological writings. After observing the Eastern Roman Empire's inability to defend the people from Lombard attacks, Pope Gregory took it upon himself to mount a defense, feed the people, tend to the injured, and organize troops that would fend off the attacking barbarians. He used diplomacy on several occasions and managed to spare Rome from being sacked again. He worked tirelessly on bringing about general peace to Italy and Europe. Central Italy lacked strong civil rulership at the time, and Gregory brought the administration of this region under the papal office, which paved the road for the establishment of the Papal States.

Pope Gregory the Great established the superiority of the Roman see above all other Western churches by meddling in their work. He claimed that the see of Saint Peter was dominant and that all bishops and monks should obey the pope, especially when it came to disciplinary measures. He also advised them to always look to Rome when in need of spiritual or diplomatic guidance. Gregory was very interested in the Anglo-Saxons after he first met them in the slave markets of Rome. He thought that such fair people shouldn't be slaves and pagans but should convert to Christianity and be bathed in the light of God. He selected a monk named Augustine to travel to the Anglo-Saxons and convert them. A new church was founded in Britain, and the pope had a personal interest in its work.

The popes weren't the only ones working tirelessly on the conversion of western Europe to Catholicism. The monks played a huge role in the events as well. They were able to help people accept papal supremacy because, with the collapse of the Roman Empire, life had shifted from the urban centers to the countryside.

Society became primarily agrarian and rural, which became a problem for the Western Church since it was mainly stationed in the urban areas. The monks were an ideal solution to the problem. Their monasteries were already in the countryside, and they had access to the heathen peasants. It was only natural for the monks to leave their ascetic cells of the monasteries and start missionary work among the folk that lived around them. So it happened that Saint Martin founded Gallic monasticism and became the main missionary who brought the faith to rural France. But perhaps the monastic movement had its greatest influence in the far west among the Celtic people. There, Saint Patrick worked to convert the nation and to found the church. Since there were no cities in Ireland, the church was founded on monastic foundations instead of urban episcopal ones.

Throughout the 6th and 7th centuries, the Irish monks were the soul and spine of the missionary work in Europe. Irish monasticism closely resembled the Egyptian one, with monks dedicating their lives to asceticism. Although they converted much of the European population, they didn't bring spread the message of papal supremacy. For that, Europe needed the Benedictine monks, who, in the 8th century, worked their mission through Europe, mainly into the territory of Germany. They were very loyal and dedicated to the papacy, and they brought the whole of Europe under the pope's sphere of influence. Benedictine monks, especially Saint Boniface, who started the Catholic Church of Germany, were also instruments in bringing the Franks into an alliance with the papacy. This alliance was the future of Europe and the foundation of Western Christendom. Saint Boniface was invited to the Frankish kingdom to reform the church, which fell into corruption. He organized a series of councils between 742 and 747, during which he created a strong discipline for the Frankish clergy and also created a strong bond between the Frankish church and the pope.

In 754, the pope and the Frankish kingdom made an official alliance. This alliance was possible because of how Rome worked. Due to Pope Gregory the Great's efforts, the pope was seen as the de facto ruler of central Italy. Still, Rome had to defend its territories, and since popes didn't have an army at their disposal and were able to recruit only a small number of people, they turned to the Franks for help. So, in 754, Pope Stephen II embarked on a historic journey to meet King Pepin the Short (r. 751–768). The king was able to guarantee papal rule over a large portion of Italy, from Parma and Mantua to Apulia. Thus, the dominion of the pope became recognized in public law as the Papal States, which remained an independent territory until 1870. In turn, Pope Stephen anointed Pepin and his two sons who would later succeed him, Carloman and Charles (better known as Charlemagne).

Charlemagne

When Pepin died in 768, the Frankish kingdom was divided between his sons. But Carloman died soon after in 771, and Charles became the sole ruler of both halves of the kingdom. Pope Stephen anointed him when he was in the company of his father during the alliance-making meeting. The pope also gave Charles the title of "Patrician of Rome," which meant he was both the protector of Rome and the pope. As such, he had to defend Rome from the Lombard attacks, and soon he had the opportunity to prove his dedication to his title. In 772, King Desiderius of the Lombards attacked the Papal States and took control of some papal cities. Pope Adrian I immediately called on Charles, evoking his responsibility to defend Rome. In 774, Charles not only defeated Desiderius and thus defended the Papal States, but he also crowned himself king of the Lombards.

Charles soon proved he didn't want to only act as the protector of the pope; he wanted to become his sovereign. He personally supervised the administration of the Papal States and even issued orders to the pope. Charles was convinced he was on a sacred mission to unite the people of western Europe under one Christian banner. This led him into countless battles on all sides of his empire. In the south, he fought against the Arabs, while in the southeast, he seized control over Bavaria. Once he defeated the Avars, he opened the way for the Franks to conquer the territory that is today's Austria and Hungary. But his greatest effort was in the east, where he fought the Saxons. This fight lasted for thirty-two years, but Charles managed to not only conquer the Saxons but also to complete their conversion to Christianity. The German plains, which stretched as far as the Elbe River, became part of the Frankish lands. Finally, Charles finished his conquest by defeating the Slavs across the Elbe.

By the year 800, Charles's realm stretched far and wide, from the Pyrenees to the Elbe River. With his conquests, Charles managed to reconstruct the political unity of the Western Roman Empire. However, his title was still king and the protector of the Romans. It remains unclear if Charles pursued the title of emperor or if he was even aware of the pope's intentions to crown him. In 800, Charles had to travel to Rome to clear Pope Leo III's name, as he was accused of adultery and perjury. Two days later, it was Christmas, and the king joined the masses in St. Peter's Basilica. There, the pope suddenly put the imperial crown on Charles's head and proclaimed him emperor. Since the coronation was performed by the pope, it was regarded as the will of God, and the new title bestowed on Charles was holy.

But Leo III had political motives in making Charles a ruler of the renewed Western Roman Empire. In doing so, he denied the legitimacy of Empress Irene, the heiress to the Eastern Roman throne in Constantinople. Since the pope thought of the Roman Empire as one and as being indivisible, he thought that Charles had the right to claim both the Western and Eastern Roman Empires.

However, Leo III achieved the opposite. By crowning Charlemagne, he managed to construct two separate claims to the Roman throne, and the empire was now permanently divided. Constantine's coronation was caused a war in 802, and in the ages to come, these two empires would try to impose their sovereignty onto each other.

Whether Charles knew about the intended coronation is not important because the renewed Western Roman Empire became a reality. There are indications that he wanted to reject the title of emperor because he feared conflict with the East. It is also possible that he didn't like the fact that the pope took the power of coronation onto himself. That was too much power in the hands of a religious leader, as it meant he was at least equal or even above the emperor.

Nevertheless, Charles couldn't refuse the crown when everyone expected him to claim it anyway. His sacred mission of uniting the world under the Christian banner was now even more feasible. The coronation was the perfect representation of the alliance between the pope and the Franks, and it united the Western world into a new social order under Christendom.

Chapter 7 – The Papacy and the Holy Roman Empire

Thomas Becket and King Henry II of England, a depiction from the 14th century.
https://en.wikipedia.org/wiki/Thomas_Becket#/media/File:Jindrich2_Beckett.jpg

The empire Charlemagne created was, in essence, a continuation of the Western Roman Empire. But at the time, it had nothing in common with the ancient empire. It had no Senate, Roman law, legions, or civic servants who would administer it. Even its capital wasn't in the city of Rome. Instead, it was a massive territorial patchwork with different land magnates and chieftains who acted as local leaders. However, the empire of Charlemagne was a concept of a united Europe as a commonwealth of the Christian peoples. This idea still needed developing, and its final shape would come into being long after Charlemagne's time.

There were many European countries, but they were all united by a common faith, intellectual culture, and a sense of righteousness and duty. Europe was a union of both the spiritual and temporal, but as such, it was a beast with two heads. It often left people confused over who had the higher authority. Was it the pope or the emperor? This question persisted through the Middle Ages and was the cause of much bloodshed.

During the reign of Charlemagne, nobody questioned his supreme authority. He made decisions of both temporal and ecclesiastical importance. But after his passing, various popes tried to impose their superiority over his successors. In their eyes, the role of the emperor was to promote Christendom and direct the people toward the final goal of the church: eternal salvation. In a manner of speaking, the popes regarded emperors as their subjects who should always strive to work for the greater good of Christendom and the church.

The Fall of the Papal Supremacy

After Charlemagne, the popes started strengthening their position by making sure the emperors understood that the crown on their heads was given to them by the successors of Peter. It was the pope who crowned the emperor and placed a sword in his hands, symbolizing the duty of the emperor to protect the faith. During the 9th century, the popes even gained the right to intervene in the state's affairs. The state was no longer a distinct political entity; rather, it was seen as one of the many aspects of the church. At the end of the 9th century, Pope John VIII managed to win the papal right not only to crown the emperors but also to choose them.

The empire of Charlemagne quickly fell apart once his descendants chose to quarrel over their right to rule. Three brothers—Charles the Bald, Lothair, and Louis the German—divided the empire between themselves. Charles III the Fat, son of Louis the German, managed to unite his grandfather's empire for a brief moment, but in 887, the Franks rebelled against him, as they considered him a German king. For the next several decades, Europe's unity was shattered by the attacks of the Vikings and the Magyars, and the age of feudalism started. The bishops considered this a breakdown of the Christian society of western Europe. As the empire slowly collapsed, the papacy was affected. Instead of rising above the political situation in Europe and leading the people once again, the papacy became a slave to the local Roman political factions. Popes were constant players in the game of political intrigue, and they lost their sense of morality and spiritual authority.

The papacy reached its lowest point during Pope John XII (papacy 955-964). He was only around eighteen years old when his family pulled some political strings to place him on the throne. He was inadequate for the position because he couldn't control Rome, and he clashed with the Lombards. In order to stop the Lombard aggression on the Papal States, Pope John sought help from the East Francian king, Otto I of Germany (r. 962-973). In return, Otto was crowned as the emperor of the Holy Roman Empire, reviving the one created by Charlemagne. Otto's empire was considered a continuation of the previous one, although it was much smaller because the Spanish and French territories weren't included. The renewed Holy Roman Empire predominantly occupied Germany, but it also reached Italy.

Otto I found it very convenient to use the church to combat disorder in his empire. He made bishops his main collaborators, as they were well educated and had no children who could claim large portions of feudal territory to develop into rival dynasties. But Otto needed the pope's support to implement the system in which the bishops occupied all of the important positions in the state. The pope was still regarded as the head of the church, so Otto reconfirmed the grants of Pepin and Charlemagne and became the guarantee of the independence of the Papal States. Of course, the pope had to abandon his claims of authority over temporal matters, and within only one year of Otto's coronation, the emperor acquired the power to dispose of the pope. The new popes who were to be consecrated had to first swear an oath of loyalty to the emperor.

Once again, the relationship between the church and the state was very intimate, and Otto's descendants continued his policy of employing bishops as the crown's officials and of making and unmaking the popes to serve their political needs. Some emperors went so far that they even believed they were chosen by God to lead the people. Their power grew so much that Holy Roman Emperor Henry III (r. 1046–1056) called a synod, the Council of Sutri, in which he got rid of Pope Benedict IX, Antipope Gregory VI, and Bishop John Gratian, who also served as Pope Sylvester III. In their stead, Emperor Henry III installed Clement II.

It wasn't only the Holy Roman emperor who was able to use the church for his own political gains. Feudal Europe created a perfect ground for the land magnates to start using the faith and their representatives as they saw fit. According to old canon law, the bishops were elected by the clergy and people, but now, this law was completely disregarded. Kings and their vassals had the power to control the appointment of the bishops. The land that bishops gained with their investiture was considered a feudal obligation, and they took precedence over his ecclesiastical duties. The candidates for the position of bishop often had to resort to bribery and pay significant sums of money to ensure their election. Ordinary churches couldn't escape the feudal system either. Laymen owned the land on which a church was built, as well as all other church properties connected to the land. They were also able to hire and get rid of the priests and clergy as they pleased.

Reform of the Papacy

There were men of faith who were still courageous enough to ask the question: how can a church, the body that was Christ's legacy bestowed upon the apostles and their successors, the popes, be subject to a layman? The loudest among these individuals who wanted change was Cardinal Humbert of Silva Candida (who died in 1061). In 1057, he wrote *Libri tres adversus Simoniacos,* in which he criticized those who bought clergy positions with money and the layman and kings who sold ecclesiastical offices. He advocated the obedience of the layman to the clergy, not the other way around. He even went as far as to claim that laymen should not obey the clergy only in the church and in matters of the faith but also outside of it in temporal matters. He reasoned that the church and the state were united in one body, that of Christendom.

But before the church could rise above the feudal system and release itself from the laymen, the papacy needed to free itself from the emperor's power. The opportunity presented itself when Emperor Henry III died, leaving a six-year-old male successor behind him. On top of that, Pope Victor died only a year later. A reformed party was organized in the Curia, the administrative institution of the Holy See of Rome. The Curia then elected Stephen IX, who was reform-minded. But Stephen soon died, and the party had to race against the nobles and elect someone else from among their ranks, Nicholas II (papacy 1059–1061). The new pope issued a decree with which he managed to exclude the emperor and the nobles from electing the pope. From then on, the pope would be elected by the cardinals, and the emperor only had the honor of confirming the election.

When Nicholas II died, his decree came to a test. The cardinals elected Pope Alexander II, but he had to fight for his right to the office. He had to go against not only the emperor but also the

Roman nobles, as well as the Lombard bishops and imperial magnates. However, complete papal supremacy over the temporal powers would only be asserted in 1073 with the ascension of Pope Gregory VII.

Gregory VII Hildebrand was known for his fiery temperament that resembled that of the Old Testament prophets. The men were easily drawn to him due to his zealous vigor and righteousness. He was elected without following the usual election protocol. This is why he decided not to accept the papal office and flee. When he was found, his election was confirmed by the cardinals and the people. Nicholas II's law that the emperor should confirm the pope's election was completely ignored, which was Hildebrand's first step toward freeing the church from the imperial iron fist. In 1075, he penned the famous *Dictatus papae*, in which he calls for papal authority in all matters. The pope would define right and wrong, and all souls who considered themselves Catholic would obey. No one was to judge the pope except God, and it was the pope's ultimate power to excommunicate or grant absolution to anyone. According to Gregory VII, the pope had the right to punish and dispose of disobedient rulers.

Under Gregory's leadership, the reformation of the papacy progressed. But this was possible mainly because Emperor Henry IV was very young and inexperienced, and he wasn't popular among his subjects. When Henry expressed his wish to continue meddling in ecclesiastical matters, a confrontation between the emperor and the pope was unavoidable. Due to the internal troubles in Germany, Henry IV accepted papal supremacy, but as soon as the danger was over, he revealed that it was all just a sham. His real intention was to make the pope a subordinate and make the imperial office above the ecclesiastical ones. The pope and the emperor deposed each other in 1076.

The papal excommunication struck Henry hard, as he soon found out he had little supporters among the German princes. They gave Henry an ultimatum: either gain the pope's absolution by February 22nd, 1077, or step down. By January, Henry met the pope in the Alps and stood in the snow for the next three days, begging for absolution.

Although Gregory VII forgave Henry IV, with the emperor being considered cleansed of his sins, his political enemies finally deposed him that same year. Rudolf, Duke of Swabia, was elected as the new emperor. Henry wouldn't make peace with the election, and the pope was invoked to make a final decision. The result was a renewed excommunication of Henry IV in 1080.

However, Henry managed to defeat Rudolf and turn the populace of Germany against the pope. Once again, Henry deposed Gregory and installed an antipope, Clement III, in his place. The emperor even came to Rome to make sure his orders were followed, and Gregory had to flee to the castle of Salerno. The pope's defender, the Norman ruler Robert Guiscard, tried to reinstall Gregory, but in doing so, he left Rome in ashes. The destruction of the city was blamed on Gregory, who now had no chance of returning. Pope Gregory VII died in 1085, overwhelmed by the events that were his doing and the doing of his enemy, Emperor Henry IV.

Gregory was dead, but his cause continued to live on in his successors. His immediate successor was neutral, as he was chosen by the emperor. But the next in line, Pope Urban II (papacy 1088–1099), continued Gregory's reforms. His efforts to emancipate the church were great, but he was more pragmatic than Gregory and would often moderate himself to appease the conflict between the state and the church. Nevertheless, the papacy of Urban II continued on the successful path set by Gregory. At the Council at Clermont (1095), the pope called upon Christian knights to join the crusade against the Muslims, in which they would free the tomb of Jesus. Urban II used this call not only to free the Christian sacred land but also to strengthen his position in Italy and to ensure papal ascendancy as the head of the Christian Church. The lords and nobles of all of Europe were enthusiastic about the holy war, and they gathered around the papal banner. With the successful rallying of men, Pope Urban II displayed how much influence over the minds and hearts of the people he had. No emperor or king could hope to topple papal authority anymore.

But the question of the clergy's election and investiture remained open. A compromise was reached in some parts of Europe, which included three main points. The clergy would elect the bishop with minimal participation of the laity; the monarch would be present, thus allowing him to assert his influence, though limited. The monarch would also invest the bishop but only his secular powers and obligations, not temporal. The temporal authority would bestow temporal powers only to the newly elected bishop, but not before he paid homage to said authority and receive consecration. In Germany, this compromise of the election was introduced during the Concordat of Worms in 1122.

The popes were able to achieve their final victory due to the dynastic changes that occurred within the Holy Roman Empire. The son of Henry IV, Henry V, died in 1125, and the throne went to Lothair III (also known as II) of Supplinburg. To secure the pope's support for his coronation, Lothair gave away control over the German bishops.

The Zenith of the Papal Monarchy

After the popes finally asserted their authority over the emperors and kings, they had to vindicate their claims of authority over the Christian Church. This is a very important claim that is still ongoing. From the 4th century until today, the popes consider themselves the heads of Christianity. The papacy has always strived to assert jurisdiction over other Christian churches, and they claimed the right to do so because Rome was the see of Saint Peter, the first Christian bishop. But other churches resisted Rome's efforts to subdue them. One such example is the church founded by Saint

Augustine in Africa, which still follows the old structure of church authority in which a considerable amount of autonomy is given to its branches and common matters are discussed and resolved during bishop meetings.

Rome developed a centralized idea of the church hierarchy, and it received its final form during Pope Leo the Great's papacy back in the 5th century. Rome was at the apex of a pyramid that enveloped the Christian churches. But the African and Eastern churches never agreed to this concept of Rome's authority, and the hierarchy envisioned by Pope Leo was at odds with their concept of ecclesiastical councils of equals. But the Western Church managed to build this pyramidal hierarchy nevertheless, one in which all the Western churches were subjected to Rome. The pope had absolute control over the Western churches.

Even after reasserting their dominance, the popes struggled to keep it alive. The emperors of the 12th century continued to challenge their authority, especially because they needed the cooperation and support of the secular rulers to appoint bishops. One such struggle came about during the papacy of Pope Alexander III (papacy 1159–1181), who clashed with Holy Roman Emperor Frederick Barbarossa (r. 1155–1190), who was considered the greatest ruler after Charlemagne. Barbarossa wanted to subdue the Lombards of Italy, but the pope would have none of that. The emperor had no other choice but to attack Rome and install his own antipope to secure the support of the church. Pope Alexander III joined forces with the nobles of the Lombard towns, and with the support of most of Europe's states, they defeated Barbarossa. But the drama didn't reach its end until Barbarossa and Pope Alexander III met at St. Mark's Square in Venice. The emperor was overwhelmed by his guilt, and he threw off his imperial insignia and prostrated himself in front of the pope's feet. The story notes that Pope Alexander wept while raising the emperor from the ground and hugging him.

At the same time, the pope had to deal with the internal problems of the church, which were connected to an individual named Thomas Becket, Archbishop of Canterbury, England. Thomas was fully committed to papal authority and the supremacy of the church. But that put him in conflict with his king, Henry II. He advocated for the rights and privileges of the church, and one of the points of the conflict was papal supremacy. The conflict escalated when Henry II issued the Constitutions of Clarendon in 1164, with which he tried to return the relationship between the church and the state to the old feudal period. The constitution severely limited papal control of the English Church. Thomas was even forced to flee England, and he found sanctuary in France, where the pope armed him with the power to confront the king and fight for the church's authority. Papal legates were sent with Thomas Becket back to England to act as arbitrators between him and Henry II. But the king chose another approach. On December 29th, 1170, he ordered Becket's assassination. All of Europe was outraged, and to save his crown, Henry had to submit to the papal legates and swear obedience to Alexander III. All his infringements on the church's authority were repealed.

Lotario di Segni was only ten years old when Thomas Becket was murdered, but he would soon grow to be one of the most powerful popes of the medieval period, Pope Innocent III. He studied theology in Paris, and he took his time to travel to England and visit the place of Thomas Becket's martyrdom. Like his hero, di Segni was devoted to papal supremacy. He was elected pope in 1198 and remained in office until 1216. He worked hard to raise the papacy to the highest possible level of spiritual and temporal authority. Innocent III was one of the finest legal minds of his time, and he wrote many letters in which he displayed his concern for the church's status. Thus, he started advancing the papacy by claiming that the origin of temporal power lies within the papal office. He took the title "Vicar of Christ," meaning he was Christ's representative on earth. Innocent III also meddled in the European political scene and played a major role in determining the continent's destiny.

The first political problem Pope Innocent had to deal with was the dispute for the imperial throne, which rose between Philip, Duke of Swabia, and Otto, Duke of Brunswick. The pope chose Otto, who in return promised he would maintain and defend the independence of the Papal States. But when war broke out, Otto proved to be a weak leader. He used an assassin to get rid of Philip and finally assumed the throne. But once he had the crown on his head, Otto broke his promise to the pope and attacked his domains. Innocent displayed his papal authority by excommunicating and disposing of Otto and placing his ward, Frederick II (the grandson of Barbarossa), on the imperial throne. Frederick was only sixteen at the time, and he issued his Golden Bull of Eger in 1213, granting the pope immense power over the German church, including the right to solely decide over the disputed appointments of bishops.

Pope Innocent III's greatest triumph over the secular leaders was his victory over King John of England. The king attempted to impose his nominee for the election of the archbishop of Canterbury. The pope had another candidate in mind, Stephen Langton, who was already elected by the clergy, but John stubbornly refused to recognize him. As a punishment, Pope Innocent III placed all of England under interdict, which meant no religious services were allowed in the country except for baptisms and funerals. The interdict lasted for six years, during which King John exiled many priests and confiscated their property. But in 1213, Pope Innocent threatened to invade England, as he had aligned with King Philip II of France. King John cracked under the pressure, as he knew his subjects wouldn't support the war. He chose to perform an act of homage and submit to the pope; he even placed the whole country under the vassalage of Innocent III.

But then a sudden switch in the drama occurred, and Pope Innocent found himself siding with King John against Stephen Langton and the bishops of England, who insisted on ending the abusive demands the king imposed on the church. They wanted the king to write a guarantee of their freedoms and rights. Finally, in 1215, John had to sign the Magna Carta, consecrating England to the government of law and not despotism. The Magna Carta was the beginning of the English constitution.

John appealed to the pope, though, and Innocent proclaimed the Magna Carta invalid. John's enemies were quickly excommunicated, and Stephen Langton was expelled from his office. King John died suddenly a little over a year after the signing of the Magna Carta, and the nation gave its support to young King Henry. Now it was Innocent's turn to reconcile with England, and he did so through the mediation of Langton.

Another European ruler had to bow to the pope's superiority, this time on the matter of morality. Philip II of France married a Danish princess named Ingeborg in 1193, but only a day after the wedding, he proclaimed he had a physical aversion toward her and demanded a separation. He also immediately started living openly with his mistress, even though he failed to procure an annulment of his marriage. Ingeborg asked the pope to give her justice, as she was unwilling to accept being an unwanted wife. Innocent III laid an interdict on France but refrained from excommunicating the French ruler because he needed his friendship in the case of war against England. Philip was thus forced to acknowledge Ingeborg as his queen, but he refused to treat her as a wife. The pope continued to refuse him a divorce, with the whole affair lasting for years. Finally, after almost twenty years, Philip fully acknowledged the Danish princess as his queen and wife, giving her all her deserved privileges and rights.

In 1215, Pope Innocent III gathered the Fourth Council of the Lateran, which had more than four hundred bishops and eight hundred priests, abbots, and foreign ambassadors present. This was the biggest medieval church council to gather, and the question of the ecclesiastical election was finally resolved and canonized. However, the council did much more than that, as the qualifications for the admission of the clergy were decided and precisely formulated, and the regulation of various details of clerical life was discussed and settled. For example, the style of dress and the acceptable recreation activities were decided and defined. Innocent also took the chance to reorganize the Papal Curia, as the office was pressured to take many more responsibilities. The Curia was divided into three parts: the Chancery (dealing with records and documents), the Camera (dealing with finances), and the Judiciary.

Chapter 8 – The Great Schism of 1054

The world divided between the Western and Eastern Churches
https://en.wikipedia.org/wiki/East%E2%80%93West_Schism#/media/File:Expansion_of_c hristianity.jpg

The relations between the various Christian sees were never completely friendly. Since the times of the Council of Chalcedon (451) when Canon 28 was accepted (where Constantinople was given the same privileges as Rome), the tension between the Eastern and Western Churches only grew. But the canon wasn't the only issue that divided the church, as political, cultural, and social forces created deep fissures between the two sees. Although the pope's view of the nature of Christ prevailed during the Council of Chalcedon, and the papacy emerged as the uncontested head of the church, it didn't last long. In 680, with the Third Council of Constantinople, Pope Honorius was anathematized for his Monothelite beliefs that Christ had a single will, separate from his Holy Father. When the Muslims seized the sees of Jerusalem, Alexandria, and Antioch, Constantinople became the head of the church. The conflict between East and West was renewed in the 8th century when the Byzantine emperors tried to enforce iconoclasm (the destruction of icons and holy images).

The Photian Schism

In 858, Byzantine Emperor Michael III deposed Ignatius, Patriarch of Constantinople, and put Photius in his place. Photius was the son of a very wealthy Byzantine family. Since Photius did not have a rank at the time, he was quickly made a monk, and then in only four days, he was ordained as a lector, sub-deacon, deacon, and priest. All so that by Christmas, he could be made the patriarch of Constantinople. This quick ascension was the opposite of the Western canon, so Pope Nicholas I had to object, especially since Photius openly refused to acknowledge the pope as the supreme leader of the church. In turn, Nicholas I refused to accept Photius as the patriarch.

In 867, the throne of the Byzantine Empire was usurped by Basil the Macedonian, who immediately removed Photius and restored Ignatius to the position of patriarch. Nevertheless, the Fourth Council of Constantinople held in 869 didn't favor the restoration of the old patriarch. The council also brought the Bulgarian Church under the see of Constantinople, although Rome had claimed it earlier.

Ignatius died soon after, and Photius was brought back. This time around, the patriarch was very eager to repair the relations between the Eastern and Western Churches. During the next Council of Constantinople, held in 879, the Bulgarian Church was assigned back to Rome (though the Kingdom of Bulgaria refused this), and the acts brought about in the council of 869 were all annulled. Rome was recognized as a true orthodox follower of the faith, and the reconciliation between the pope and the patriarch was completed.

The whole of the 10th century was relatively peaceful, and the popes maintained good relations with the Byzantine Empire and with the patriarch of Constantinople. But that didn't mean that the East and West managed to resolve their issues; they were still there, lying dormant. These issues were raised once more by the Western Roman Empire's revival and its transformation into the Holy Roman Empire. Otto I the Great imposed a German influence over Rome, and with it, a new reform, originating in the north of Europe, entered the Holy See. This reform included the addition of the Western *Filioque* to the Creed. The main idea of the *Filioque* clause is that the Holy Spirit was the product of both the Father and the Son, as the Latin phrase bore the meaning "and from the Son." Until that point, canon stated that the origin of the Holy Spirit was only in the Father (God). Although *Filioque* has its origins in Spain, it eventually traveled to the Carolingian court, and from there, it was passed to German clergy, who then brought it to Rome. Around the year 1000, it became a part of Rome's official doctrine.

But the East was offended by *Filioque*, as the priests and patriarchs of Constantinople saw it as a disturbance in the balance of the Holy Trinity. They were adamant on keeping the nature of the Holy Spirit true to the old definition, in which it originated from the Father *through* the Son, never *from* the Son. But the question of *Filioque* was also a question of ecclesiastical supremacy. Would the authority of the church belong to the patriarch or the pope? This was far too great a question to be decided easily, and both the East and West were aware that only a new council would be capable of answering it.

Mutual Excommunication

The Eastern Church didn't have a defined attitude toward the claims of supremacy by the papacy. They thought of ecumenical councils as the only bodies that could inspire a doctrinal authority. That means that if the West added something new to the Creed issued by the council, the authority of that council was not respected. Only another council could change or add to the Creed and determine the right way in which the church should move. Everything else was considered heresy, and it didn't matter if the popes claimed authority of the church.

But the Great Schism was yet to happen. The peoples of the Christian faith were very supportive of each other, and no matter the nuances of their faith, they were closely bound by Christendom. This bond between the Christians only strengthened during the early 11th century when many people went to pilgrimage in distant Jerusalem. They traveled together to avoid the loss of material goods and lives due to road bandits. Because of this unity in Christendom, many efforts were made to repair the relationship between the sees in Rome and Constantinople.

In 1024, with the support of Byzantine Emperor Basil II, Patriarch Eustathius proposed a formula that would acknowledge Rome's supremacy but leave Constantinople with a significant amount of autonomy. Although the pope agreed, the monks who supported the Cluniac Reforms, which tried to bring back the old monastic life to Western monasteries, declined this proposal. The pope was pressed to withdraw his acceptance, and the East and

West remained estranged. The political situation in the south of Italy only served to aggravate the situation.

Around 1020, the south of Italy was under Byzantine control, but many of the noble houses disagreed with the political setup. They started a revolt against the Greeks and even invited the Normans, who were passing the territory on their way to pilgrimage, to help them. The revolt didn't result in liberation. Instead, the Norman knights turned against the nobles and started conquering southern Italy. The pope didn't want to react, though, as the Normans were defeating the Byzantines. Rome was pleased because at least these Normans were Catholics and faithful to the papacy.

But the Normans didn't stop with banishing the Byzantines; they soon turned to threaten the Papal States. In order to suppress them, Pope Leo IX approached the Byzantine emperor in his search for an ally against the Normans. However, this alliance never came to be because the Byzantines wanted their territories in southern Italy back, and the pope wasn't willing to give them away now that they had become Catholic.

In 1053, the conflict escalated when the pope demanded that the churches in southern Italy conform to Latin practices. If they refused, the pope ordered them to be shut down. At the time, the patriarch in Constantinople was Michael Cerularius, who did not have the diplomatic affinities of his predecessors. He was a very arrogant and spiteful man, but he had the support of the populace. Instead of approaching the papacy to resolve the conflict, he chose to shut down all of the Latin churches in Constantinople. He also sent a letter to the bishop of Trani (in Apulia, southern Italy), saying he should refuse to conform to the Latin practices, especially the use of unleavened bread during communion. The patriarch also made sure that the pope received a copy of this letter.

Under the influence of the Byzantine emperor, Michael Cerularius wrote to the pope, again asking for Christian unity instead of conflict. But the pope found himself offended because the patriarch of Constantinople addressed him with "Brother" instead of the usual "Father." Moreover, his translators failed to interpret the word "Oikumene." Instead, they claimed that Michael Cerularius had signed as the "Ecumenical Patriarch," which would imply that Cerularius claimed authority over the whole church. At that point in history, the Greek word "Oikoumene," which the patriarch used, meant only "empire." And Cerularius indeed signed the document as the "Patriarch of the [Byzantine] Empire."

Pope Leo IX sent papal legates to Constantinople with letters for the patriarch and the emperor. Among these legates was Humbert of Silva Candida, who had no love for the Greeks and was deeply offended by the reception the patriarch had organized for them. Cerularius, on the other hand, was offended by the pope's need to even send the legates in the first place when all he wanted was to repair the relations between the two sees. He refused to recognize the papal legates as officials from Rome, and he didn't want to deal with them at all. But Byzantine Emperor Constantine IX received Humbert, and the papal legate felt encouraged to publish some documents criticizing the Greek practices and defending the Latin ones. One Eastern monk found Humbert's writings offensive, and in turn, he started defending the Greek practices and attacking the Latin practice of celibacy. Angered, Humbert raised the question of *Filioque*, but Cerularius continued to ignore him.

Having no more patience, Humbert and his associates strode into the church of Hagia Sophia (now Holy Hagia Sophia Grand Mosque in Istanbul, Turkey) on July 16th, 1054. They timed their arrival to be right before the afternoon liturgy, and they laid their excommunication bull on the church's altar. The bull targeted Patriarch Michael Cerularius, as well as Emperor Constantine IX and all their followers and supporters. Furthermore, the bull accused the Byzantines of simony (selling of the church offices), rebaptizing the Latin followers in Constantinople, allowing priests to take wives, refusing communion to men without beards, and much more. All of these were untrue or half-truths twisted to fit the narrative Humbert was pushing.

The citizens of Constantinople rioted, as they were, of course, offended by such accusations by the papal legates. The emperor had to order a public burning of the bull to appease his people. A synod gathered and condemned the actions of Humbert and the other papal legates. The blame was put on the legates as individuals and not on the pope. Humbert and his associates were excommunicated by the patriarch, but the patriarchate in the East allowed the pope to resume peaceful negotiations.

However, at the time, nobody knew that Pope Leo had died before the legates even reached Constantinople, which means they acted entirely without his authority. The next pope in line could have easily renounced the actions of Humbert and saved some prestige, but that didn't happen. Humbert was popular in the West, and his description of the events in Constantinople was accepted as a triumph. The future Pope Gregory VII (papacy 1073–1085) was even a personal friend with Humbert and gave his support. Every bishop in the West believed that the papal legates did the right thing by excommunicating the patriarch and the emperor. Eventually, the excommunication was extended to the whole Patriarchate of Constantinople.

The East-West Schism

By 1081, Gregory VII had excommunicated Byzantine Emperor Alexios I Komnenos, further degrading the relations between the East and the West. But hope still existed, and the people of the period didn't consider this conflict to be a schism. When Urban II, a man who despised controversy, was elected pope, he started reconciling with the Byzantine Empire. To show the goodwill of the papacy, he lifted the excommunication of Emperor Alexios, and in response, Alexios gathered a synod in Constantinople, which found out that popes and Roman bishops were "accidentally" erased from the Eastern diptychs (lists of names of individuals who are commemorated during the liturgy). Even though the emperor urged that the pope be returned to the diptychs, the Eastern Church wanted Urban II to make a conciliatory gesture and earn the honor. However, the pope didn't feel the same, so he remained off the Eastern diptychs. But even this didn't stop the sees of Constantinople and Rome from resuming good relations.

Urban II made a call for a crusade in 1095, which he hoped would serve the reconciliation between the West and East. All those of the Christian faith were invited to join a holy war against the Muslims and free the Eastern Church. The pope also hoped that the past conflict would be forgotten and that he would emerge as a leader of all Christendom. But that didn't happen. The Crusades had a very different effect from the one Urban II hoped to get. Instead of uniting the Christians, the Crusades only served to divide them even more. When the city of Antioch was conquered in 1098, the Byzantine emperor and the Western knights quarreled about who should control it. The hatred between the Eastern Christians and the Western knights started to run deep, and the leaders of the Western knights drove the patriarch of Antioch into exile. In his place, they installed a Latin patriarch, which caused a schism in the East. This schism was only the beginning of a far greater one, in which the Eastern and Western Churches would be divided forever.

It is impossible to give the exact date of the Great Schism, although the year 1054 is taken as the starting point when the attitude of the Eastern and Western Churches became obvious. The event that finally ended all hopes for reconciliation was the Fourth Crusade (1202–1204). Even though this crusade was called by Pope Innocent III, Byzantine Prince Alexios IV Angelos managed to persuade the knights to help him gain the throne of Constantinople. The knights accepted because they lacked the funding to reach Jerusalem and because they had previously been excommunicated for sacking the Latin Christian city of Zara (modern Zadar, Croatia).

When Alexios proved himself an inadequate ruler, the populace deposed him. But that meant he had no money to pay the Crusaders who helped him get the throne. Angered, the Western knights decided to conquer Constantinople. The result was the fragmentation of the Byzantine Empire in 1204 and the foundation of the Latin Crusader States, which occupied ex-Byzantine territories. The people of Constantinople were outraged that their empire crumbled, and they could never forget or forgive what the Western knights had done. The schism between the Greek and the Latin churches was now definitive.

The papacy tried to heal the schism on two later occasions, at the Council of Lyon in 1274 and the Council of Florence in 1439. But these efforts had political motives rather than Christian, so they were bound to fail. The emperor of Constantinople and his patriarch accepted reconciliation nominally but never did anything to implement it. The first serious steps toward true reconciliation were made in the modern period during the Second Vatican Council (1962–1965). One of the goals of this council was to unify all Christians and seek a pardon for Catholic contributions to the separation of the churches. The result was the Catholic-Orthodox Joint Declaration of 1965, which was issued in both Rome and Istanbul. According to this declaration, the mutual excommunication that took place during the Great Schism was annulled. That didn't mean the end of the schism, but it did birth the hope that the two churches could work together in the future.

Chapter 9 – The Decline of the Papacy

Pope Innocent III
https://en.wikipedia.org/wiki/Pope_Innocent_III#/media/File:Innozenz3.jpg

With the fall of the Roman Empire, religious learning in the West was reduced to distant monasteries and endless copying of religious texts. But an intellectual awakening occurred at the end of the 11th century, and soon European cultural life would change forever. In 1170, the first universities were opened, at first around the cathedrals of northern Europe. But gradually, the universities gained a life of their own and became the vital centers of learning.

At first, learning was available only to future priests, and the main subjects taught were theology, law, medicine, and ecclesiastical history. But in the late 12th century, with the renewed popularity of Aristotle's writings, the learned people tried to harmonize the human experience with faith. The most successful among them was Thomas Aquinas (1225-1274), who managed to synthesize the rational thought advocated by Aristotle with the Gospels. His work titled *Summa Theologiae* represents the peak of the intellectual achievement of Christendom of the 13th century.

With the discovery of the complete works of Aristotle, the Christian thinkers were challenged by the rationalistic interpretation of the human existence. This is because Aristotle was a very diverse ancient Greek writer who touched upon themes such as zoology, botany, astronomy, law, physics, ethics, logic, political science, and philosophy. But most of all, Aristotle used ration as the starting point for all of his writings, which was something the medieval Christian thinkers had never encountered before. The popularity of Aristotle grew even more with the discovery of Arabic commentators, who emphasized the lack of religion in his writings. At first, the ecclesiastical authorities banned the development of a rational way of thinking, and the works of Aristotle, especially in the universities of Paris and Oxford, were banned in 1210. But eventually, the ban was lifted because it was impossible to stop hungry European minds from learning.

By the middle of the 13th century, the study of Aristotle and rationalism was incredibly popular. Christendom reached its golden age under the leadership of the popes, who followed Hildebrand's idea of supremacy over the church. The intellectual, artistic, and spiritual achievements of Christian Europe were immense and even affected the political shape of the continent. The 13th century saw the rise of national monarchies and the decline of imperial authority, but the emperors wouldn't allow the fall to be theirs alone. They brought the papacy down with them.

The Conflict with the Hohenstaufens

Pope Innocent III deposed Emperor Otto IV in 1215 and personally selected his ward, Frederick Hohenstaufen (Frederick II, King of Sicily from 1198, King of Germany since 1212, Holy Roman Emperor from 1220 to 1250), as the new emperor. The pope wanted to keep Sicily apart from the Holy Roman Empire so that the emperor wouldn't claim that he had a right to rule all of Italy. Although Frederick promised that Sicily would never join the empire while he reigned, he proved to be the popes' most dangerous adversary. The conflict between the popes and Emperor Frederick II proved to be a disaster for both the empire and the papacy.

At first, the relations between Frederick and the papacy were good. In 1213, he issued a golden bull by which he confirmed the integrity and independence of the Papal States. He also freed the German church from imperial control and guaranteed free episcopal elections. As a reward, the pope crowned Frederick Holy Roman emperor in 1220 in Rome. But soon, Frederick made his move against the towns in Lombardy, which, in the eyes of the pope, was a step away from attacking the Papal States. Pope Honorius III (papacy 1216–1227) didn't do anything about it, but his successor, Pope Gregory IX (papacy 1227–1241), reacted aggressively. He excommunicated Frederick, seemingly for delaying the crusade that he had earlier vowed to participate in.

The pope also proclaimed a crusade against Frederick, but the pope was at a disadvantage since he had no army. He tried to call the Lombard cities to his cause, but they were busy fighting among each other. Frederick didn't inspire loyalty among the German princes, and he had a standing army of only fifteen thousand men. The majority of Italian cities were able to withstand such an army, so the pope was able to defend his properties with the little army he had managed to gather. However, the major conflict didn't break out yet; there were only a few small skirmishes. The pope and Frederick made peace, but the emperor didn't give up on his aspirations to conquer the Lombard cities. In 1238, he attacked them again and angered Gregory, who excommunicated the emperor once more.

Pope Gregory IX died in 1241, and the meeting of the cardinals who were to choose his successor lasted for the next two years. Finally, a successor was elected: Pope Innocent IV. The new pope was previously friendly toward Frederick, and the emperor was relieved, as he hoped Innocent would lift his excommunication. But that didn't happen. The new pope realized Frederick strove to reduce the church to servility to the empire. Innocent chose to buy some time for the papacy by pretending to negotiate. In 1245, he traveled to Lyon, where he called a general church council, during which he proclaimed Frederick a heretic and an oppressor of the church and confirmed his excommunication.

In response, Frederick attacked Italy, but the war soon spread through Germany, and the whole of Christendom felt the consequences. All over Europe, cities and towns were engulfed in conflict as two factions rose to power: those who supported the pope and those who were loyal to the emperor. In the cities of northern and central Italy, these factions were known as the Guelphs and Ghibellines. For a long time, it seemed that Frederick would win, even though the pope was using all of the church resources to fight him. The pope used not only an army but also spiritual weapons, such as indulgences for anyone who would stand against Frederick. In 1248, Frederick suffered a great defeat at Parma. Although he managed to recover and continue the fight, he died in 1250, and with him died the dream of the Hohenstaufen dynasty subduing the church.

It became even more important now to keep Sicily and the Holy Roman Empire separate political entities, and to do so, the Curia had to find a new king for Sicily, one that wouldn't have imperial pretensions. The successors of Frederick, Manfred and Conrad, were thus out of the question, as they belonged to the Hohenstaufen dynasty. The answer was found in France. Charles of Anjou, brother of King Louis IX of France, proved to be the perfect candidate. Charles had no claims on the imperial throne, and he promised that he would defend Sicily and keep it an independent kingdom. The Curia was even more relieved when the imperial crown passed to Rudolf of the Habsburg dynasty in 1273.

In the meantime, Charles of Anjou had to fight Frederick II's sons for the crown of Sicily, and he was victorious. He defeated Manfred, who previously staged a coup in Rome against Pope Urban IV. The Hohenstaufen successor died in battle in 1266. Two years later, his sixteen-year-old brother Conrad was captured and beheaded in Naples. This was the end of the Hohenstaufen dynasty, and the popes could now proclaim their final victory.

However, this victory came at a high price. The spiritual weapons they used against the Hohenstaufens lowered the papal prestige and the authority of the office. This decline of authority increased when a revolt against the French rule occurred in Sicily. Charles of Anjou had never been welcomed there, as Sicilians resented the French. The pope embarked on a crusade against the revolting Sicily, and the War of the Sicilian Vespers (1282–1303) started. The result was a crushing humiliation for the papacy. Once again, the Curia used everything to suppress the freedom-loving Sicilians: money, the army, and spiritual weapons such as excommunication and indulgences. But it was all for nothing. The people of Europe watched in dismay, and the papal authority crumbled. The war in Sicily dragged on for years.

National Sentiment

In 1294, Boniface VIII became the pope. Boniface was a man who had an exalted sense of papal authority. He revised the canon law and proclaimed the first papal jubilee in 1300. Millions of pilgrims were drawn to Rome, which Boniface hoped would elevate papal prestige, but that didn't happen. His other actions ensured that the papal prestige declined even further. He constantly meddled in the affairs of individual dioceses, and he pursued political alliances and conquests to ensure the guarantee of independence for the Papal States. Like his predecessors, Boniface was persistent in imposing a papal vassal as the Sicilian ruler, but he failed to achieve this. Furthermore, the pope acted as the arbiter of European affairs in international politics, imposing papal authority over the whole of Europe. He was able to do so because, with the fall of the Hohenstaufen dynasty, there was no one strong enough to oppose the pope. But this would soon change as a new political idea started gaining momentum across the continent: nationalism.

At the start of the 14th century, the idea of Christendom was replaced with a new theory: the largest autonomous political unit in Europe should be a national state. This idea was promulgated by the monarchs, who managed to influence public opinion and build up their power by promoting a sense of belonging to one nation. They did this to shake off the papal yoke and rule as they saw fit, not as the pope ordered them. The most notable monarch at the time was Philip the Fair (r. 1285-1314), King of France. Philip was a tyrant, and he had only one goal in mind: the creation of the French nation. Philip started a conflict with Pope Boniface soon after he was crowned, and the turning point of the conflict was clerical taxation. Philip needed money to consolidate his power, and the church's wealth was an attractive target. He imposed heavy taxes on the clergy, which resulted in Boniface's *Clericis laicos* (issued in 1296), a bull that declared the secular monarch needed papal approval for the additional taxation of the clergy.

Philip was forced to compromise with the pope, but he remained determined to place the church into servitude to the state. In 1301, the bishop of Pamiers was arrested on counts of treason, heresy, and blasphemy. It was very apparent that King Philip was behind the arrest, as the two were bitter opponents since the bishop had acted as the papal legate who protested the king's anti-clerical measures. Philip violated clerical immunity and put the bishop on trial. Boniface had to react, and he issued yet another bull, *Ausculta fili*, making it clear to Philip that a king was subordinate to the church. In the bull, the pope listed the crimes of Philip the Fair and invited the French bishops to attend a council in Rome.

Philip made a clever decision to appeal to the national sentiment of his people instead of openly challenging the pope. Public opinion became Philip's ultimate weapon against papal authority, and he knew exactly how to manipulate it. He forged a papal bull in which Boniface allegedly claimed direct temporal authority over the monarch. Once this false bull started circulating among the people, they were outraged, thinking that the pope was arrogant. Philip then proceeded to call a general meeting of nobles, bourgeois, and French clergy, hoping they would condemn Boniface. With his persuasive and manipulative powers, he managed to gain the assembly's support. In response, the pope issued his famous bull, *Unam sanctam*, in 1303, by which he proclaimed papal supremacy over Christendom in Europe.

But Philip wasn't concerned, as he had the support of the public. He simply issued an order for the arrest of Pope Boniface VIII, accusing him of being a materialist with a highly immoral soul who neglected to fast, indulged in sexual misconduct, kept a demon as his advisor, and much else. Philip's order targeted Boniface as a man, not the papal office, and because of this, he was able to gain the people's support.

Boniface decided not to go down without a fight. He established himself in his native city, Anagni, where he perched on a high cliff. There, he was protected by his private guards, and he prepared the bull that would officially excommunicate the king of France. But Philip was quick, and he dispatched his henchman, Guillaume de Nogaret, and 1,300 armed soldiers to bring the pope to France. After a day of fighting, Nogaret's force managed to break down the doors of the pope's house and arrest him. The townspeople of Anagni organized Boniface's rescue, preventing Nogaret from taking him away. The pope was already in his eighties at this point, and he wouldn't survive for much longer, especially due to the stress of these events. He was dead within months.

The events that followed Boniface VIII's death only served to confirm Philip's victory over the papal office. The next pope in line was the archbishop of Bordeaux, who was crowned Clement V. At the time of his election, the new pope was still in France, where he was established in Lyon. This new pope proved to be no match to King Philip, who arranged for his detention in France. He blackmailed Clement by saying he would stage a posthumous trial for Boniface if he ever left the country. He then used the pope's position to coerce a condemnation for the Knights Templar from him. This occurred during the Council of Vienna in 1312, and it was the most scandalous defeat from which papacy ever suffered.

The Pope in Avignon

Since Clement V was trapped in France, he decided to move the papal court to Avignon in southern France in 1305. Thus, the Avignon period of the papacy began, and it lasted until 1378. This new arrangement only brought greater decline to papal authority.

Avignon was a perfect choice for a new see because it was well protected by the fortified walls, and it was close to Italy. The French city was only supposed to be a temporary residence while the conflict with the French king played itself out. However, Avignon would be the residence for seven popes altogether. Many factors influenced their decision to stay: the continuous war in Italy, the intrigues of the French court, the health issues some of the popes had, and the continuation of the struggle with the Holy Roman emperors.

By the time of Clement's death and the succession of John XXII in 1316, war raged in the Papal States. The states already suffered from the complete exhaustion of the apostolic treasury, as the previous popes had indulged in various extravagances and wars. The Curia was disorganized because of the pope's long absence. If the papacy was to remain the head of Western Christendom, drastic measures needed to be taken. The popes in Avignon tried to influence the situation by reorganizing the church's administration. Their efforts were tireless, and their main goal was to increase papal authority and influence throughout the Christian world. They strengthened papal control over the appointment of clergymen, even at the level of parishes. They also tried to reform church life and revive the practice of devotion to work, study, and poverty. But many of their reforms only had an impact on nearby locales due to the influences of secular rulers, the constant wars, and the Black Death, which spread across Europe at the time and decimated its population.

The 14th century was a period of great disorder in Europe. Aside from the fact that the plague depleted the ranks of the clergy, many warring parties saw monasteries as perfect targets. They would attack, kill the monks, violate the nuns, steal their food and relics, and burn their fields. It was during this period that many European monasteries perished.

The Avignon popes tried to govern the church effectively in these times of great disorder, but they lacked the funds. To come up with the money, the papacy in Avignon established various new taxes and fees that targeted the bishops, abbots, and priests. Papal collectors were sent all over western Europe to collect the taxes, especially in those places that had no papal representatives present. Those who failed to pay were ruthlessly excommunicated. But with such taxation policies, the popes lost their popularity, and many tax collectors were hunted down, thrown into prisons, and even murdered.

The Avignon popes felt the need to display the church's wealth, which they hoped would inspire the people to support the papacy. They built an enormous palace in Avignon, trying to display all the pomp and magnificence of the age. The spacious rooms of the new palace were filled with knights, chamberlains, courtiers, squires, and various seekers of fortune. Even the most prestigious courts of Europe looked up to the pope's palace in Avignon as an example of luxury. In fact, the pope's palace was thought to be the most civilized court in the world, and it attracted many scholars, artists, and pilgrims. But it seems that while the popes were building their earthly residence, they completely forgot to dedicate their time and thoughts to the spiritual world. The Avignon popes were certainly not spiritual-minded men who would spend their lives in conformity to the Gospels.

The popes always intended to return to Rome, but the Papal States were under rebellion, and at that time, the pope was not welcome in Italy. In 1352, Pope Innocent VI (papacy 1352-1362) found a talented general in Cardinal Gil de Albornoz and tasked him with reinstating the papal rule in the Papal States. This was to be a tremendous effort since the states were almost disintegrated. Albornoz led his small army of mercenaries to Italy with very limited resources. This was a time when gunpowder became a popular choice for warfare, and the soldiers needed to be equipped with muskets and guns. Cardinal Albornoz displayed incredible skill and courage and managed to subdue the rebellious Papal States, at least to a certain degree. Campagna showed immense resistance, and Albornoz died before he could quell the rebellion there. Still, the pope was so grateful that he appointed him the legate of Bologna.

Pope Urban V was the first of the Avignon popes to enter Rome, doing so on October 16th, 1367. Unlike the other Avignon popes, Urban followed the rules of monastic life, living humbly and without pomp. Although this didn't secure him the support of the cardinals and bishops who were used to living extravagantly, papal prestige increased significantly. Pope Urban V strove to reform the church through the introduction of changes in its administration and through the promotion of patronized learning. He restored many schools, granted privileges to universities, and even opened a university in Hungary. He also donated the church's wealth to revitalize many monasteries throughout Europe. Urban also wanted to work on reconciliation between the Eastern and Western Churches. Although he established good relations between them, he didn't succeed in bringing the two together.

But during Urban V's pontificate, discord broke out in Rome. Several cities of the Papal States were still rebelling, and the French cardinals urged the pope to return to Avignon. Urban was unable to resist them because although he had gained the support of the people, the Roman nobility didn't want him there. Urban returned to Avignon in 1370, and after only a couple of months, he died. His successor, Gregory XI, realized that if the pope remained in Avignon any longer, his control over the Papal States would be lost forever. Although he returned to Rome, he died in 1378. He, too, was unable to strengthen the position of the papal office in Italy.

The Papacy Survives the Schism

When Gregory XI died, the Roman people were afraid they would lose the papacy to Avignon because French cardinals predominated the Curia, so it was highly possible that a French pope would be elected. This fear led to many people attacking the cardinals who were gathering for the election. The cardinals were wise enough not to antagonize the people of Rome, and the next in line for the papacy was an Italian, Urban VI (papacy 1378-1389). But though he was Italian, the new pope proved to be a tyrant, especially to the cardinals who elected him. He would accuse them of treachery, simony, and living life in luxury. This behavior expanded from the cardinals to the whole church, bringing about what is known as the Western Schism (or the Papal Schism).

The schism began when thirteen cardinals, who were accused of misconduct by the new pope, decided they had enough and abandoned Rome. They issued a manifesto, in which they proclaimed Pope Urban VI's election was invalid. In the manifesto, they called the pope the anti-Christ, a tyrant, demon, and so on. The dissident cardinals attracted the support of Queen Joan of Naples and other cardinals. On September 20th, 1378, they elected a new pope, Clement VII.

Both popes had the support of civil governments since politics played a large role in what was happening in the church. Thus, the Western Church was divided into two groups of supporters. The Holy Roman emperor and the kings of England, Poland, Netherlands, Portugal, and Hungary gave their support to Urban, while France, Scotland, Austria, and Luxembourg stood firmly behind Antipope Clement VII. Some kingdoms claimed neutrality, but they would change their alliances if they saw they could gain benefits for their own political goals.

The popes soon proclaimed a crusade on each other, and war ensued. The English king, intending to break the French allegiance to Clement, decided to cross the Channel and invade France. However, the military operations proved to be very expensive, and the papal tax collectors implemented even harsher methods of collecting taxes. Papal popularity hit a new low, which only made Urban more violent. He suspected the cardinals who remained loyal to him, and he often tortured them; he even killed five of them! Pope Urban died in Rome in 1389, and his cardinals hurried to elect his successor, Boniface IX, to deprive Clement of the papal throne.

The Avignon pope, Clement VII, died in 1394, and Christendom hoped this would end the schism, even more so when the candidates promised they would resign from office if they were elected. But the successor in Avignon, Benedict XIII, soon proved he had no intentions to honor his promise, which only made France turn its back on the Avignon papacy. The result was a long battle between the pope and the French king, cardinals, and bishops, who all strived to change Benedict's mind. The battle lasted for five years. The pope's palace was even besieged, all without success. France lost the battle against the pope and returned to being an obedient subordinate.

Hope arrived in 1406 when Gregory XII became the Roman pope. He seemed willing to restore the unity of the church, and he promised he would resign if the Avignon pope resigned too. The French again stood up against their pope, and Benedict knew that he would not win the battle this time around. He agreed to negotiations with Gregory, but both popes proved to have very different intentions. Gregory claimed he could not travel to Savona, the city chosen for the meeting. Benedict, on the other hand, moved on Italy with an army. The two popes never met, and the cardinals finally decided to take the matter into their own hands. They summoned a council with the idea of introducing conciliarism into the Western Church. The basic principle of conciliarism was that a council would have the power to gather in times of extreme necessity and reach a decision without the pope's consent. The council also had the power to issue decrees that didn't need the pope's approval.

This new concept of conciliarism was revolutionary for the church of the early 15th century because up until then, the popes always had supremacy over the councils of cardinals. However, it seemed there was no other way to mend the schism. On March 25th,

1409, the cardinals of both factions gathered in Pisa, where the church officials performed a ceremony of summoning the popes. But since the popes were still in their respective cities, it took only but a moment for the church officials to declare them schismatic heretics and guilty of bringing grievous scandal upon the church. The council and the universal church proclaimed both popes to be deposed. The cardinal of Milan was elected as the new pope, and he took the name Alexander V.

But it was too early to celebrate. The two other popes were still very powerful and held allegiance over a large part of the church. Moreover, Alexander V died in Bologna in 1410; he did not even manage to reach his see in Rome. The next year, his successor, John XXIII, entered Rome with an army. He took control over the Holy See and summoned a council, but few cardinals showed up. John was famous for nepotism and a luxurious lifestyle, which alienated many of his supporters.

New hope came not in a spiritual but a secular leader. Holy Roman Emperor Sigismund (r. 1433-1437) dedicated himself to mending the schism because he desired a unified Christendom and Europe. He persuaded John XXIII to agree to call a universal council in 1414 at Constance, but John entered the city, riding a white horse, covered with a golden canopy, followed by fanfare, and escorted by his cardinals and courtiers. All of Western Christendom was represented in this council, but Pope John was the only one displaying his prestige.

Because Pope John managed to fill the council with his followers, Emperor Sigismund decided to change the voting rules and divide the council into nations. Five nations were recognized as dominating the Catholic world: Germany, Italy, France, Spain, and England. The right to vote was extended not only to the clergy but also to professors of theology and law and some representatives of the noble houses. Each nation was to gather an individual assembly and do the first round of voting. After this assembly reached an agreement, another round of voting would be performed, where each nation would have a single vote.

Pope John had no intentions of allowing the council to outmaneuver him. Although he promised he would renounce the papacy if the other two popes would do so, he soon escaped the council and took refuge with the duke of Austria. The council decided to continue the voting even in the absence of Pope John because healing the schism and reforming the church was more important than one individual.

The Council of Clermont confirmed the conciliation. This decision humiliated all three popes, and their followers soon started deserting them. Pope John had no other choice but to return to Constance, where the council put him on trial and deposed him. Pope Gregory XII resigned the office as promised, ending his papal career in dignity. But the pope in Avignon, Benedict XIII, resisted. The council had no other choice but to excommunicate him. The court of Aragon continued to recognize Benedict XIII until his death, but the schism was basically over. The council chose a new Roman pope, Martin V.

Papal Triumph Over Conciliarism

The council took some time to discuss whether a new pope should be elected immediately or if they should first work on reforming the church. Many feared that the new pope would block the reformation if his heart was inclined to preserve the already existing situation in the church. Finally, the council reached a compromise. They would choose a new pope but not before they issued a decree that would guarantee that the pope would oversee the implementation of the reforms. On October 9th, 1417, they issued Frequens, a decree that obliged all future popes to call a meeting of the council regularly. They also passed a new method of electing a pope, with each nation sending six delegates, thirty in total, to join the cardinals in the voting. Pope Martin V was the first one elected in this way.

The council managed to heal the schism and unify Western Christendom, but they failed at implementing the administrative reforms in the church. The schism infected all branches of the church, from tax collectors to courts. The bishops were corrupt and often absent from their bishoprics, and the clergy indulged deeply in immoral behavior. Simony was everywhere, even in the Roman Curia. The council recognized all of these abuses and was willing to deal with them, but they were unable to persuade everyone to completely eradicate them. The core problem was that each group wanted to implement reforms upon another group, but when it was their turn to reform, they would simply refuse to do so.

To repair the schism, the council reorganized itself to fit the narrative of the nations. This was a success, but the very notion of the nations proved to be a problem in implementing the reforms, as the nations often fought each other. It took the council only one year to pass the reform decree, and even then, it was an extremely vague and general reform that would limit papal power and condemn simony and the sinful conduct of the clergy. Other reforms were left to the pope to resolve, in agreement with the individual nations. But for this to happen, the pope and the council would have to work in harmony. Unfortunately, the popes were often in conflict with the council.

Martin V knew that if he was to be taken seriously and regain some of the papal authority, he had to return to Rome. However, it took him two years to enter the city, which was left in disorder and disarray. Before he could reform the church, the pope had to repair his city. He invested enormous amounts of time and money in repairing the streets, bridges, and public buildings of Rome. Alongside this tremendous work, Martin V managed to return the Papal States under the control of the papal office. But he spent all of his time preoccupied with the games of war that the Italian noble families were playing. Martin proved incredibly successful on the Italian political stage, but he failed to implement the reforms in the church. If he had somehow managed to do it, he would have healed the discord between the papacy and the council and maybe even prevented the Protestant Reformation, which would bring about a new division of the faith.

Historians often rush to put the whole blame on Pope Martin V. However, if he had concentrated all of his power on reforming the church, the history of the Italian Peninsula might have turned out completely different. In any case, the council was disbanded in 1424 without achieving anything significant. Martin's successor, Eugenius IV, tried to take the next step toward the reformation of the church, but from the very beginning, he was opposed to conciliarism. Even though he ratified the council that gathered at Basel in 1431, he soon found himself aligned against it. The pope found it difficult to concentrate on the council because of many national unrests that were occurring around the borders of the Papal States. The Hussites (proto-Protestant Christian movement) were manifesting themselves, and the Greek Orthodox showed their interest in the workings of the Catholic council. Already aged and with fragile health, Eugenius decided to call off the council at Basel.

This proved to be a grave mistake. Germany was begging for immediate reforms, as their clergy was already at the lowest possible standard, and new heresies threatened to erupt. The members of the council refused to give up, and they defied the pope and even threatened another schism. But Eugenius was stubborn, and the council had no other choice but to declare itself superior to the papal office. Two months later, they ordered Eugenius to show up at Basel. This defiance of the council was the climax in the struggle against papal authority and the start of a revolution within the church. At first, it seemed that this revolution would succeed and implement the reforms even without the pope's approval, as the reforms had the support of fifteen out of twenty-one cardinals. Even the Christian rulers of Europe were on the side of the council. In 1433, the pressure on the pope was so great that Eugenius issued a bull, *Dudum sacrum,* by which he annulled his previous attempt to dissolve the council. He even recognized all the rights of the council.

The council in Basel was now free to implement all of the reforms. But just as before, the individual groups, whether national or ecclesiastical, refused to implement the reforms on a more personal level. However, they all agreed that the papacy needed reforming. The council was eager to work on the fiscal abuses of the Roman Curia, and they took away the papal right to collect taxes and issue indulgences. This was too much for Eugenius, though, as these reforms would make him just a mere figurehead, and the papacy would be financially dependent on the council. Thus, he could not agree to this radical move. Instead of reforming the papacy, the council only managed to alienate it. But at the time, the pope couldn't do much but wait.

The right moment soon presented itself. The Byzantine emperor was pressed by the Ottomans and relied on the West for help. Eugenius considered this to be the sign that the time was perfect to reunite the Eastern and Western Churches. But for the next two years, the pope, the council, and the Greeks couldn't agree on a place for the meeting. While Eugenius wanted to meet in Italy, the council and the Greeks pressed for another place, one outside of the pope's area of influence. The Greeks were the first to give in to the pressure, and they agreed on the pope's choice of a city in Italy. In 1437, the council voted, and the majority decided not to leave Basel and move to Italy.

Many bishops were disgusted by the behavior of their fellow council members, and they joined the pope, whose position started growing stronger. The council was finally transferred to Ferrara in Italy. In 1439, those who remained in Basel decided to depose Eugenius and install a new pope, Felix V. This was the last antipope in the history of the Catholic Church. Regardless, Eugenius triumphed against the council at Basel, for on July 5th, 1439, he officially declared the reunion of the Eastern and Western Churches. The event was celebrated across Europe as a great achievement, and the pope was announced as the one true Vicar of Christ and the head of the Christian Church. However, the reunification fell apart once the Eastern Church refused to ratify the pope's decree. Nevertheless, the pope proved he was stronger than the conciliarists.

One by one, the European rulers declared their allegiance to the Roman pope. France was the first to do so in 1438, followed by Aragon and Scotland in 1443. The final blow to the council at Basel was the Concordat of Vienna, which was signed in 1448. In it, the Holy Roman emperor personally ordered the Basel members to abandon the council. Antipope Felix resigned the next year.

Despite all the odds, the papacy managed to defeat conciliarism. But in its efforts, it failed to reestablish the moral and spiritual leadership over Catholic Christendom.

Chapter 10 –The Reformation and the Split Christendom

Sale of indulgences, woodcut from 1530.
https://en.wikipedia.org/wiki/Martin_Luther#/media/File;Jeorg_Breu_Elder_A_Question_ to_a_Mintmaker_c1500.png

Constantinople was conquered by the Ottoman Empire in 1453, and the fall of the city resonated with the whole Christian world. Aeneas Sylvius Piccolomini (who later became Pope Pius II), a papal legate, expressed his worry that the fall of Constantinople was just an overture to the fall of Christendom. He believed, as many of his contemporaries did, that both the pope and the Holy Roman emperor became empty titles. Neither of them had the authority or the power to lead the Christian community into a brighter future. Every nation had its king or prince, and they all played a political game, neglecting their faith in the process. Although the Papal Schism was healed, and the pope triumphed over conciliarism, he never managed to regain his authority or at least his popularity among the people. But it wasn't only the papacy that was suffering. The church as an institution had rotted on all levels. Decay and disorganization were the main problems, and if it wasn't addressed soon, the church would be no more.

At the top of the church was the Roman Curia, which, at the time, was in a major scandal. In fact, the wickedness of the Curia was a constant theme of 15th- and 16th-century literature. All the evils that came to the church originated in the Curia. The cause of the scandal was simony. In the 15th century, the whole system of the Curia and the church itself functioned through simony. The popes had the right to appoint a large number of ecclesiastical offices, and selling them to the highest bidders was a lucrative business. It is estimated that by the time of Pope Leo X (papacy 1513–1521), there were around two thousand ecclesiastical offices for sale, and the Vatican was selling them. Those bishops who wanted to buy the position of archbishop had to pay immense taxes to the pope. To collect enough money, they were selling indulgences, and they still had to give a percentage of their earnings from indulgences to the Curia.

Another odious practice was the ability for one man to buy multiple offices. Certain rich individuals did this to combat the rising inflation of the 15th century and continue living their lives of luxury. But the plurality of the offices resulted in absenteeism. Many of the bishops never stepped into their diocese, and church morale greatly suffered. The lesser priests started abusing their power and neglecting the administration of their churches. The church offices were also in the hands of the high nobility. Many princes paid for their younger sons to become men of religion so they could continue living as aristocrats, even though they would not inherit their father's riches. Some of these sons were as young as eight when they became bishops. As such, they were unable to provide their diocese with spiritual leadership.

The lower clergy was hardly in any better shape. Besides the usual corruption, nepotism, and sinful conduct, there was simony, a practice that was greatly used by ordinary priests. To sell more offices, the Curia came up with "mass priests," whose sole purpose was to say daily Mass. In large cities, the mass priests constituted around 10 percent of the population. These priests had no formal education in theology; rather, they were extremely ignorant and superstitious. Only a small number of priests had a university education, and even they would often indulge in sinful behavior.

Even the monasteries suffered from decay. The Benedictine doctrine was hardly followed, and the abbots were usually absent, leaving their monasteries to the secular administration. Monasteries were no longer places of education, and many monks lost touch with modern society and culture. The monastic community was dead, and there were no more communal prayers. The monasteries gave up on their common property and gave in to personal possessions. The monks even went as far as to ask for the pope's permission to live outside their monasteries, and for the right amount of money, they were able to gain it.

The Reform Ideas Before Martin Luther

The church needed reform, and most of the bishops were aware of it. But they didn't know how to achieve it since the councils in Constance and Basel had failed in their attempts. Yet, they saw no other way but to form another council, this time under the pope's leadership. That council never managed to meet because the

Renaissance popes of the 15th century were more interested in European, more specifically Italian, politics than in leading the church. From the outside, it looked as if the Renaissance was the pinnacle of the papal office, as Rome was the capital of the world. After all, Italy was the birthplace of the Renaissance. The pope was its biggest patron, which made the papacy look like a grandiose and divine office. However, if one scratched the surface, they would find moral and spiritual decay. Renaissance popes such as Sixtus IV, Innocent III, and Alexander VI were some of the most corrupt men to hold office. They bought their way into the papacy, and they used the office to promote their personal and dynastic interests. They promoted their sons and relatives to the positions of cardinals, disregarding the fact these people had no formal education or dedication to the faith.

Politically, the Renaissance popes were some of the most successful statesmen. Pope Julius II (papacy 1503–1513) elevated the Papal States to become leaders in European politics. Julius chose his name in honor of the ancient Roman Emperor Julius Caesar, and he was nicknamed the Warrior Pope. He preserved the independence of the Papal States during the Italian Wars, and his contemporary, the scholar Erasmus of Rotterdam, described him as intending to conquer heaven if Saint Peter denied him entry. Even the famous Niccolò Machiavelli described Pope Julius II as the perfect prince, completely disregarding his spiritual role and concentrating only on his political power.

Finally, in 1512, Julius II called the meeting of the Fifth Council of the Lateran, but he died a year later. His successor, Leo X, continued the effort and concluded the council in 1517. A reform program was drawn, and it mainly focused on the ignorance of the clergy, the papal obsession with world politics, and the centralization of the bureaucracy. The constructive solutions for these problems included training and education for the clergy, the revision of the canon law, and calling a regular ecclesiastical council every five years. However, Leo X found these reforms too spiritual, and he was unwilling to implement them. Although the council had come up with some good solutions on how to combat the spiritual decay of the church, the pope did nothing to promote the reform, and nothing was accomplished.

Some of the clergymen who called for the reforms in the first place had different ideas on how they should be implemented. They were unwilling to rely on the pope, who they rightfully saw as a leader sitting in the most corrupt ecclesiastical office. They believed the reforms should start from the bottom, with the pious and devoted monks, priests, and missionaries. In their eyes, these people had the power to set an example of sanctification and apostolic activity and move their religious orders and parishes to implement reforms. This method of reform was slow and humble, and it meant a return to the communal monastic life, common table and prayer, and modest way of living. Such orders existed in the 15th century; among them were the Franciscan Observantines led by Bernardine of Siena and John Capistrano, the Dominican Lombard congregation, and the Augustinian monastery of which Martin Luther was a member. But even these orders failed to implement the reforms simply because they lacked the support of the church leaders.

Secular princes also attempted to reform the church. The Saxon dukes received papal permission in 1485 to reform the monasteries on their territory. The French kings used their great power and prestige to subdue the church and persuade its leaders to implement some changes. However, the Spanish rulers were the only ones who managed to make a real and large step toward the complete reform of the church. The Spanish spiritual leaders, priests, and bishops were almost all pro-reform. Even the archbishop of Toledo, Ximenes (Jiménez) de Cisneros, led an ascetic life, and he dedicated most of his forty years in power to reform the Spanish Church. Under the leadership of Ximenes, the

Spanish king and clergy learned how to collaborate without fighting for authority. They promulgated the new teachings, which combined the reform ideas and the tradition of the Spanish Church. This made it much easier for everyone involved to accept the reforms.

Another pre-Lutheran reform effort deserves mention. It was promulgated by the Christian humanists. In the late 14ᵗʰ century, starting with Francesco Petrarca (better known as Petrarch; 1304–1374), the Humanism movement began. This was an artistic and intellectual movement that advocated history and critical thinking. The main weapons of the humanists were satire, criticism, and irony, which many writers of the 15ᵗʰ century often used in regard to the church. These weapons ridiculed the practices and beliefs of the faith and served to instill a dose of skepticism toward the church. The humanists wanted to reform the church through education, assuming that learning would inspire piety in people. They believed knowledge could make people better, not worse. But that was an optimistic view of human nature, and history would eventually prove them wrong. The humanists were reckless in criticizing the church and the traditional Christian way of thinking.

The humanists' insistence on the historical aspect of Christianity made them victorious in implementing some of the reforms they envisioned. They urged theologians to constantly improve their knowledge and to learn ancient languages so they could study the original sources, such as the Bible and the lives of the fathers of the church. Furthermore, scholars had to implement methods of historical criticism in their studies to follow the latest humanist and Renaissance cultural trends. The greatest humanist Christian scholar was Erasmus of Rotterdam, whose study of the Greek New Testament (1516) and the church fathers would serve as textbooks for later patristic scholars.

To sum up, there were many reform ideas before Martin Luther existed, from individual Christians, both clergy and laymen, to communities and organizations, and even intellectual movements. But their reform ideas never reached the top of the papacy itself. This would only happen after the Council of Trent (1545–1563). But the failure of all these reform ideas is most likely what set the foundation for Luther's Reformation.

Martin Luther

Martin Luther was born in 1483 in the German town of Eisleben. He was born in a peasant family but raised in traditional religious practice. He was a fast learner and was sent to the University of Erfurt, the largest in Germany at the time. In 1505, he finished his studies, and several months later, he expressed his wish to become a monk. He made this decision out of fear. On his way home from the university, a lightning bolt hit the ground near him. Martin was extremely afraid of death, and he vowed he would enter a monastery. Soon, he dedicated himself to the Augustinian order and started a life of daily prayers, study, meditation, and fasting. He was so devoted to the sanctity of monastic life that his superiors took a liking to him, and he was ordained a priest only nineteen months later (in 1507).

Martin Luther chose to continue his studies of theology, which only made his spirit suffer. The peace he found in the sanctity of a monastery was disturbed, as he had learned of what the church had become. Nevertheless, Luther continued his theological career and took a position of a teacher at the University of Wittenberg and later at Erfurt. Martin traveled to Rome in 1511, and although he was disappointed with what he saw there, he didn't allow the image of the Eternal City to influence his theological development. In 1513, he finished his doctorate studies at Wittenberg and took over the office of a professor of biblical theology, a position he would hold until the end of his life.

The complete turnover in Martin Luther's theology occurred accidentally. As he described it, while reading the Gospels, the phrase "Justice of God" took a new meaning in his mind. He now knew that he didn't just need to lead a righteous life to receive salvation. Martin's new view of the Justice of God meant that it was God who, through his mysterious ways, implemented justice on the people. A man had little to do with it, and his role in gaining salvation was a passive one. Righteousness comes from Christ, as it is not in man's nature. In Martin's view, man had a corrupt soul because of the original sin. But to deserve God's justice, one must accept Christ.

Luther realized that the church had a different view on justice and righteousness, as it sold indulgences that promised one's sins would be forgiven. This was contradictory to his new revelation. Luther became more and more aware of the terrible state of affairs in the church. However, he didn't think that the church needed a revolution, at least not until he realized that the Gospels were at stake. He realized that the corrupt church was betraying the teachings of Jesus and the apostles and had replaced it with its own teaching that heaven could be bought for the right price.

Indulgences were the main source of finance for the papal office. Soon it became the official doctrine that indulgences could be applied to souls in purgatory if a living relative or friend were willing to buy it for the deceased. Before this, the selling of indulgences also included at least some level of repentance. But now, it was clear that they became quasi-automatic salvation and a ticket into heaven. A German commissioner for indulgences, named Johann Tetzel, particularly irked Martin Luther with a poem. In it, he explained how one could rescue the souls of his loved ones and send them to heaven with only a few coins.

The popes justified the selling of indulgences with the need for money for the rebuilding of St. Peter's Basilica. They twisted the selling of indulgences, saying that people were making donations to the project in return for an indulgence, which was close enough to a good deed or penitence for committed sins. One indulgence, in particular, was the main cause of Luther's wrath. The archbishop of

Mainz made a deal with the Roman Curia and the Fuggers, a German banking family, to raise ten thousand ducats through the sale of indulgences. He needed this money to buy the dioceses of Magdeburg and Halberstadt. This would place three archbishoprics in his hands, securing him a good life.

Although it is believed that the story of Martin Luther nailing his *Ninety-five Theses* on the door of Castle Church in Wittenberg is only a legend, he certainly sent his list to his bishop. It was only when the bishop in Wittenberg failed to respond that Luther made his demands public. His main goal was to inspire his university colleagues to discuss indulgences and to understand how dangerous they were for the spiritual integrity of Christendom. Luther was also a parish priest, and as such, he observed indulgences as an obstacle to the true repentance and personal conversion one needs to go through to experience salvation. He preached that the popes had no power over the human soul and that they were not in the place to promise salvation in the name of Christ and the saints. Finally, Luther condemned all clergymen who sold indulgences, as they led people to believe the wrath of God could be appeased with a few coins.

Luther considered himself a loyal Catholic, and he spoke out as one. He never intended to form a new sect or even start a revolution. His initial idea was to give his *Theses* to the church to evaluate them, as he believed the church was competent in implementing change. He didn't call on the German nation to rise up, although he did challenge the papacy. Thesis number 82 asks why doesn't the pope rescue all the souls in purgatory for the sake of Christian love if he had such power.

When no one was willing to debate Luther's *Theses*, they were translated from Church Latin to the German language, and they started circulating among the people. Sides were formed quickly, and those who opposed Luther openly avoided meeting him in debate. They didn't care to debate him; they only cared about the loss of money that his preaching would cause. The archbishop of Mainz was the first to report Martin Luther to Rome.

Pope Leo X, who was preoccupied with Italian politics, showed no interest in the matter of Luther and his *Theses*. However, he soon realized how serious the whole affair was, and he summoned Luther to show up in Rome and answer the charges of heresy. The pope was forced to assume a more conciliatory stance toward Luther due to political circumstances, though. Frederick III (1463–1525), Prince-Elector of Saxony, supported Luther's vision, and he even offered him protection. The Papal Curia needed Frederick to prevent a Habsburg from becoming the Holy Roman emperor. Due to this, Pope Leo tried to secure a quick recantation from Martin Luther so that controversy could be avoided. Luther agreed to a meeting, during which he challenged the papal authority but didn't agree to abandon his *Ninety-five Theses*. In 1518, he appealed for a general ecclesiastical council.

Pope Leo X was deep in the intrigue of Italian politics, and he allowed Luther's revolutionary idea to rest. In the next two years, nothing happened. Luther, on the other hand, used this time to indulge in public debates and gain public support. He presented his theological views as an alternative to the Roman ecclesiastical system, and this appealed to the majority of the German populace. This is where Humanism helped Martin Luther since it preached the historic and human nature of the church instead of the traditional divine and sacred origin the church claimed to have. Luther even publicly admitted he no longer believed in the divine origin of the papal office. For him, only the Scripture had supreme authority in religion, and this later became the core belief of the Protestants.

The pope was obliged to react, and he organized a commission that would study the writings of Martin Luther and help him decide on further actions. After the commission's report, the pope issued a bull, *Exsurge Domine*, in 1520, by which he condemned Luther's

Theses, proclaiming them heretical and scandalous. But the German populace would not hear of it, and they proved ready to revolt to defend the propositions and teachings of Martin Luther. On his part, Luther responded by proclaiming the pope the anti-Christ. He used his talent for propaganda and the newly invented printing machines to reach distant hamlets. He issued three manifestos, in which he addressed his countrymen and inspired a revolution in them: *To the Christian Nobility of the German Nation, On the Babylonian Captivity of the Church,* and *On the Freedom of a Christian.* He even went as far as to publicly burn the pope's bull, further antagonizing Leo X, who finally excommunicated Luther in 1521.

Although Luther and his teachings were banned throughout the Holy Roman Empire, he continued to inspire the people. The free cities of Germany were the first to declare a new religion, and they were soon followed by the prince-electors. Of course, most of the princes had their own personal or political reasons for accepting Lutheranism, but that didn't matter, as the idea of church reform finally spread through all ranks of the population, secular and ecclesiastical. The majority of European leaders hoped that reconciliation would occur swiftly. But theologists couldn't even agree on what was the main issue dividing Catholics and Lutherans. While some thought indulgences and the corruption of the church were at the center of the discord, many claimed the root of the divide was in the doctrine. For example, Erasmus of Rotterdam considered that the main issue was free will, which Luther claimed people didn't have. Luther himself claimed that the main problem lay in the proper understanding of Christ.

The Consolidation of Protestantism

Holy Roman Emperor Charles V spent the years between 1521 and 1530 involved in Spanish politics, and he was absent from his empire. This was one of the most critical periods in history, and the empire was left without its leader. Perhaps this was one of the reasons why the schism that split Western Christendom between Catholics and Protestants progressed so quickly. The conflict between the two factions escalated to the point where they started taking up arms. One of the main factors that escalated the conflict was the German Peasants' War (1524–1526). The German princes believed that the peasants rose up to express their Protestant principles. Some of the German princes were Lutherans themselves, and they took up arms to defend the peasants. In 1531, the Protestant princes organized the Schmalkaldic League, which only served to introduce politics in matters of the faith.

The next year, in the Peace of Nuremberg, Emperor Charles recognized the league, even though he was a devoted Catholic. Once he realized how endangered the Holy Roman Church was, the emperor became determined to save it. Not even the popes had the resolution and will that Charles displayed in his efforts to preserve the medieval universal Christendom. The emperor's fight lasted for the next twenty years, and he often alternated between the use of military violence and diplomacy in theological conferences. The dialogue he initiated between the Lutherans and the Catholics reached its peak in 1541 at Regensburg, where the divided Christians came very close to an agreement.

The Protestants wanted Catholics to make four main concessions: to allow clergy to marry, to offer communion in two forms (with leavened and unleavened bread), freedom from papal jurisdiction, and the freedom to perform communion without the ritual of transubstantiation (the mystical conversion of bread and wine into the body and blood of Christ). Rome showed no interest in meeting the Protestants' demands. But the fault for the failure of the Regensburg meeting wasn't only on Rome. Other countries that attended the meeting would not allow the agreement to be reached. France, for example, benefited from keeping Christendom apart. Although an agreement wasn't reached in Regensburg, the complete failure of Charles's efforts to make peace between the two factions came with the Peace of Augsburg in 1555. This peace legally recognized Protestantism and Catholicism as two separate faiths. This sealed the schism, and the idea of reconciliation was dead.

Soon after, Luther's ideas crossed the borders and spread across the continent. People proved to be very receptive to his thoughts, but many enthusiasts added their ideas to Luther's and split Protestantism into many factions; there were now Calvinists, Adventists, Baptists, Pentecostals, and many more. But ultimately, it was the monarch of a certain country who decided whether Protestantism would gain momentum. They were the ones with the power to legalize it or persecute its followers. The best example of a ruler's decisive influence is in England, where ecclesiastical reform was taken to a higher level. Henry VIII, a staunch Catholic, had a personal dispute with the pope over his wishes to divorce and started the Church of England. His son, Edward VI (r. 1547–1553), would advance the ideas of Protestantism even more. Soon the *Book of Common Prayer* and the Forty-two Articles became the foundation on which the Church of England built its faith.

Chapter 11 – Catholic Church Regains Spiritual Elán

The Council of Trent, painting by Pasquale Cati.
https://en.wikipedia.org/wiki/Council_of_Trent#/media/File:Council_of_Trent_by_Pasquale_Cati.jpg

From the very beginning of the church, it had to face exceptional challenges, such as persecution, schisms, Arianism, various barbarian invasions, and the fall of civilization. But it seems that it was Luther's revolt that brought the church down on its knees. Never before had the clergy abandoned their churches in such great numbers. Monks and nuns left their cloisters, and many altars had to be closed. It all happened almost overnight, and once it was over, half of Europe stopped paying respect to the Roman See. The unity of Christendom was nothing more but a fading memory.

But even in that darkness, certain individuals kept their optimism and were able to see the light. During the 16th century, these individuals led the Catholic Church through a spiritual renewal and revitalized the elán of its members. The Lutheran revolution split the church, but it also made the popes realize how urgently the church needed reformation. The Catholic leaders had no other choice but to abandon their old way of life and devote themselves to deepening their spirituality.

The Origin of the Renewal

In 1497, in Italy, a new movement was founded called the Oratory of Divine Love. It first started in Genoa, and it was dedicated to personal and individual spiritual renewal through religious devotion and acts of mercy. The members of this order were both laymen and clergymen. Many similar groups sprouted around Italy at the beginning of the 16th century, and one even managed to penetrate the Roman Curia. There, the heart and soul of the reform movement was a Venetian cardinal named Gasparo Contarini. When Pope Paul III appointed a commission for the reformation of the church, Contarini was chosen as its leader. Together with his friends, Contarini formed Spirituali, a reform movement with the same ideas of personal spiritual growth. One of the prominent members of Spirituali was Michelangelo, the artist who painted the Sistine Chapel.

But a more direct offspring of the Oratory of Divine Love was a new religious order called the Theatines. The founders of this order were Gaetano dei Conti di Thiene and Gian Pietro Carafa (who later became Pope Paul IV). Previously, they were the members of the Oratory's Roman branch, but their idea that the reform must begin with the parish clergy separated them from the rest of the movement. Their main objective was to install secular priests who excelled in the humble way of life and who were poor, chaste, and obedient. They thought this would raise clerical spirituality. Their idea found an audience in Italy, and it started spreading and influencing similar orders, such as the Somaschi, the Barnabites, and finally the Jesuits, which was the most successful order of them all.

The Jesuits started as a small band of men gathered around a priest named Ignatius Loyola. In 1534, he founded the Society of Jesus (Jesuits) in Paris. In 1540, the order received papal approbation in Rome, and the order was moved to Italy. Other movements had their presence in the reformation scene of the church, such as the Capuchins, who wanted to return the Franciscan order to its original ideals. Their order spread rapidly among the monks, and soon the sight of their square hoods was a common occurrence on the streets of Italian cities. They were as numerous as the Jesuits, and their influence on the Catholic Reformation was of similar intensity.

All of these movements and religious orders had initial success in reforming the various aspects of church life. They reorganized the parochial administration, monastic communities, missionaries, liturgy, and preaching. But the greater problems the church faced, such as doctrinal confusion, ignorance of its clergy, fiscal abuses, and sinful behavior, was too much for these movements and orders alone. The main problem was that each order worked on a local level, and they had no access to the highest positions and the Roman Curia. Another general council was needed to tackle these problems. But the church took its time, and no council was called for twenty-eight years after Luther's revolt. The main reason the popes didn't want to call such a council was their fear of conciliarism. But some of the members of the Curia also blocked the council since they opposed the reformation. The secular rulers proved to be hostile toward reformation too, and the church was also involved in the political rivalry between France and Spain.

The Council of Trent

It was Pope Paul III (papacy 1534-1549) who summoned the council, opening it on December 13th, 1545. The northern Italian city of Trent was chosen as the place of the meeting of around thirty bishops. This council is remembered as the heart of the Counter-Reformation, and it took eighteen years to complete its mission (from 1545 until 1563), although the council was only in session for three years. The first session ended in 1547, and this was the point where Holy Roman Emperor Charles V gave up on his efforts to reconcile the church by dialogue alone.

A ten-year interlude between the first and second sessions occurred, during which a new generation of political leaders appeared in Europe. They were less concerned with the problems of the faith. But the next pope, Paul IV (papacy 1555-1559), was energetic about reforming the church, and he advocated direct papal action in the workings of the council. However, his short pontificate didn't allow him to do much, and his successor, Pope Pius IV, quickly returned to the previous papal policy. In the end, though, he summoned the council for its third and final session.

The main task of the Council of Trent was to tackle the doctrinal confusion and the organizational breakdown of the church. A series of important decrees were issued, all accusing Luther of heresy and drawing a sharp line between Catholic and Protestant teachings. The faith of the church lay in the Scripture and tradition, and that was the official stance of the council and the papacy. On the issue of justification (the Justice of God), the church took a hard stance and refused to make a compromise. The bishops denied that man was completely corrupted by the original sin. In their opinion, faith alone wasn't enough for one to achieve salvation. A person also had to have hope and perform charity works with God's grace. They also asserted the divine validity of the seven sacraments, kept the traditional teaching of transubstantiation, and claimed the divine origin of the priesthood and the sacrificial character of the Catholic Mass.

Not all Catholics agreed with the Council of Trent's doctrinal definitions. But these individuals weren't able to do anything about it. The council was extremely conservative, and they wouldn't allow the liberal Catholics to speak. Thus, the bishops attending the council made sure that they were the ones deciding on the training that future priests would receive, making it very traditional. They paid no attention to the new ideas of the biblical studies that humanists promulgated.

When it came to the church's structure, the bishops at the council assumed the same traditional stance. They affirmed papal supremacy, but they also went further than that. They asked the pope to give his approval to all of the decrees the council brought forward, thus strengthening the papacy's grasp over the church. The bishops were given absolute power over their diocese, as they answered to no one but the pope. The laity now had no right to meddle in the church's administration. This means that the Council of Trent created a highly authoritarian and centralized institutional structure. Since the church was deeply rooted in tradition, at its core, it remained very much medieval.

In the everyday life of the church, the Council of Trent probably influenced the ritual of Mass the most. A commission was organized with the task of reforming the old, medieval way of conducting Mass, where each priest was able to add his own eccentricities and superstitions to the ritual and rob the people of the feeling of participation. This commission issued the *Missale Romanum*

(Roman Missal) in 1570, a book of the Roman liturgical rites that remained unchanged until the 1960s. The commission obliged the priests to adhere to the most minute prescriptions of the new Mass. The council's conservatism can easily be seen in the *Missale Romanum*, as they didn't even bother to introduce the vernacular into the liturgy, something that Protestants already did. The truth is the bishops couldn't admit that the Protestants might have been right about some things. That would be a disaster for the church's influence in European politics of the period. But more importantly, it would shake the claim of the Catholic Church's divine authority.

The new Mass was very traditional, and it served to unify and standardize Catholic religious expression around the world. The Tridentine (Traditional) Mass also emphasized the stability, clarity, and unity of the Catholic doctrine. However, it also deepened the feeling that the Roman Church was unchangeable, that the church would be stuck in the past no matter how modernized the world became. And it is this stubborn unchangeability that produces confusion in modern times. But above all, the new Mass failed to include the people in it. The people still had no sense of participation, and they were forced to seek devotion outside of the church to satisfy their spiritual needs.

But despite its conservatism and traditionalism, the Council of Trent played a crucial role in the Catholic Reformation. It displayed the willingness of officials to repair what was wrong inside their religious institution and let the spiritual energy run through the church once again. The key doctrines of the Roman Catholic Church were strictly defined, and reform was finally taking place. The Roman popes were at last dedicated to the cause, and they were the main force behind the implementation of the reforms. Without them, the council's decrees would have remained dead letters on paper.

Reform Popes

The first and probably the greatest of the reform popes was Pius V. He was a shining light of papal morality, and he set such standards for the conduct of future popes that the office never again suffered a serious relapse to the old behaviors of the early Renaissance popes. He was an ascetic who loved to pray. He set out to transform the Vatican from a glorious and pompous city into a monastery. Although he was at first reluctant to resume the council, he later published the Catechism of the Council of Trent, which contained a summary of the Catholic beliefs and practices. But his most important endeavor was the systematization of the Curial bureaucracy. The offices were no longer sold to the highest bidders, simony was prevented, and order was returned to the highest administrative institution of the papacy. Pius V was truly determined and even heroic in his contributions to the church reforms, and that is why he was so successful.

Even his successors continued the reform of the church, though at a slower pace. Gregory XIII (papacy 1572-1585) reformed the calendar and entered the pages of history. He was an ascetic like Pius, but his administration was fixated on continuing his predecessor's reforms. Gregory appointed a committee of four cardinals to oversee the execution of the Trent decrees. The next pope, Sixtus V (papacy 1585-1590), initiated many urban renewal programs, and he brought Rome back in order. Though Sixtus was overly ambitious (some of his big ideas never came to pass, such as the conquest of Egypt), he zealously hunted down the bandits and common criminals that roamed the Papal States. However, he was less ambitious in punishing those who committed crimes against the faith. He also gave in to the old habits of abusing fiscal power, but he did so to finance the reforms.

With the reforms enforced by the Roman leaders of the church, it became evident that the popes once again had firm control over the matters of religion. Their domain was now much smaller, as western Europe was divided between Catholics and Protestants, but the popes exercised influence they hadn't seen since the Great Schism.

One of the greatest weapons the popes had to exercise their power was the Inquisition. At first, the Inquisition was a medieval creation, and it fell into disuse (except in Spain) until Pope Paul III revived it in 1542. The Roman Inquisition suppressed heresy throughout Italy and Spain, and no one was out of its reach. Even the archbishops and cardinals could be arrested and imprisoned if they were suspected of heresy.

The Jesuit Mission

Ignatius Loyola created the Jesuit order, and it was a force that would transform the Catholic Church and shape its history in the centuries to come. He molded the spirituality of his order on his own religious experiences, which are summarized in the *Spiritual Exercises,* published in 1548. This little book was nothing more than a set of meditations, prayers, and Loyola's personal contemplations, but it had the power to change the personal spirituality of the people. It soon became an instrument of the Catholic Reformation to install a life of prayer and the belief of the apostolate in the individuals who served the church.

The Jesuits saw their service to the church as a higher calling that would ultimately serve God. They proved to be very flexible and able to provide the church with any service it needed. But in doing so, the Jesuits dropped the traditional religious practices to put themselves completely at the church's disposal. This meant that they didn't practice daily prayers according to a fixed schedule. Still, they challenged all the traditional practices of the Catholic Church and kept only those that would help them achieve their main goals: preaching, teaching, giving sanctuary, and administering the sacrament.

By 1556, the Jesuit order spread across the Catholic countries of Europe and numbered around one thousand members. They were teachers, professors, founders of schools, builders, writers, confessors, and many more. As their numbers grew, they carried out the mission across the borders of Europe and across the seas. They worked tirelessly, and their efforts came to fruition the most in Germany and Poland, which were brought back from Protestantism to the Roman Church.

Peter Canisius (d. 1597) was probably the most famous Jesuit next to Loyola himself. He was even named the second apostle of Germany. He issued his own Catechism in Germany, and he published it in different forms to appeal to people of all ages and spiritual levels. Catholicism in Germany was defined by Peter's book, which was printed in 130 editions. He also founded the universities of Innsbruck and Munich, which became centers of promoting the Catholic renewal. The Jesuits became the main ministry of Catholic colleges, and by the time of Ignatius Loyola, they controlled around seventy-four colleges across three continents.

The Jesuits are probably most famous for their work on spreading the Gospels across the world. They saw teaching and the conversion to Christianity as charity work that would secure their salvation. They first went to Asia, but they weren't very successful there, except in the Philippines. The Asians proved too conservative and unwilling to conform to the new religion's demands. In Latin America, the Jesuits had much greater success, especially during the 17th century. New missions were opened in Colombia, Peru, Mexico, and Bolivia. During the 18th century, the Jesuits thrived in the Indies and had their main seat in Goa.

The European colonial countries such as Spain and Portugal didn't approve of Jesuit missions in America. They were perceived as intrusive and an obstacle to the establishment of the colonies. In fact, the Jesuits often defended the Native Americans and prevented them from becoming slaves. They formed Christian city-states, the so-called "reductions," by which they tried to protect the natives from the colonial enterprises while at the same time converting them to Christianity. In general, Jesuits were dedicated to their missions, and they studied local languages to bring the gospel closer to the natives. Many of them constructed glossaries and dictionaries and sometimes even Latin scripts for these foreign languages.

However, the great colonial powers strove to suppress the Jesuits, and in 1773, Pope Clement XIV gave in to the pressure and suspended the order. The Jesuits still continued to work, especially in Prussia and Russia, where the secular rulers decided to ignore the pope's decree. Finally, Pope Pius VII decided to revive the order. In 1814, he issued a bull with which he reversed the suppression of the Jesuits, and the society started growing again. The Society of Jesus still exists. Its first member to become the pope was Jorge Mario Bergoglio, who took the name Francis upon the start of his pontificate in 2013.

The Revival of Catholic Spirituality

The Counter-Reformation resulted in a new type of spirituality among the Catholics. The Tridentine decree on justification explains God's justice as the cooperation between man and God. This doctrine is completely opposed to the Protestant teaching that faith alone is enough to receive salvation. For the Catholic Church, justification is bound to the act of baptism and the acts of mercy and charity that one performs throughout their life by the will of God. The decree also encourages meditative prayer, but this clause was directed toward the clergy to reform their way of thinking. Meditation was already popular as it was promoted by individuals such as Loyola, Saint Francis de Sales, and Saint Vincent de Paul.

The Catholic Church started insisting on God's grace as a priority, even above one's activity and piety. To enforce this sentiment, emphasis was put on the seven sacraments of the Catholic Church: baptism, confirmation (chrismation), Eucharist (communion), marriage, penance, anointing of the sick, and holy orders. All these sacraments were canonized at a much earlier date, but the Council of Trent confirmed them, and the Eucharist became one of the main characteristics of Catholicism, with laymen receiving communion and confessing their sins once a week. In medieval churches, communion and confession were performed once a year.

The Tridentine spirituality that now centered around the Eucharist demanded strict self-discipline, control, and regular prayer from its practitioners. But in nature, it was a humanist spirituality, as its main thesis was that man was responsible for his own faith. It was up to the people to decide how they would conduct their lives. Many new religious schools sprouted from this humanist understanding of spirituality, such as the Salesian, Carmelite, and Oratorian schools. One of the most popular leaders at the time was Philip Neri (1515-1595), the founder of the Oratorians. He combined his love for life and cheerfulness with deep and personal spirituality. This is why he had an extraordinary influence over the people of Rome, no matter their social status. Neri was also the confessor of the popes and the cardinals, which means he had direct influence over the Roman Curia's transformation.

The Carmelite school had its origin in Spain, where it was founded by Teresa of Ávila (1515-1582) and John of the Cross (1542-1591). Both of them were very gifted in literary skills, which they used to define the various stages of mysticism. Teresa was the first to scientifically define the life of prayer, which started with meditation and ended with the mystical marriage. The Salesian school was founded by Francis de Sales (1567-1622), who was the bishop of Geneva. He worked tirelessly on winning the people of the Chablais Alps district back to Catholicism, in which he was extremely successful. One of the followers of Francis de Sales, Louise de Marillac, founded the first Catholic female religious society named Sisters of Charity in 1633. The society gathered nuns who dedicated their lives to working with the poor and sick.

The revival of Catholic spirituality manifested itself not only through religious orders and the works of individuals but also through theological and intellectual ideas. The birthplace of these new thoughts were European universities in Paris, Salamanca, and Rome. Central to these new ideas were the teachings of Thomas Aquinas, who gained enormous popularity thanks to the Jesuits who spread his word across the world. The theologians of these famous universities entered debates with the Protestants and started defending papal prerogatives and infallibility. These defenders of the Catholic faith used the humanist approach to tackle the matter. They gathered historical evidence from conciliar and patristic documents. However, their work wasn't immune to Trinitarian opinion, and they often indulged in speculations of the nature of grace.

The renewed spirituality also took the form of missionary work, which can especially be seen in the work of the Jesuits, who crossed the oceans in the 16th century and started spreading Christianity through Asia and the Americas. Catholic priests followed the explorers, and aside from spreading the faith, they also played a significant role in how Europe started regarding itself toward the rest of the world. Catholic missions were established in Africa, where they flourished throughout the 16th century.

At the end of the century, the mission reached China, where the scientific knowledge of Matteo Ricci impressed the high officials. But he needed to adjust the Christian message to accommodate the Chinese ideas of religion to convert them. The Chinese easily accepted Christianity because Ricci's methods of teaching did not demand them to renounce their whole culture and, with it, the Chinese identity. But Pope Clement XI (papacy 1700–1721) banned Ricci's methods, preventing the Chinese from practicing their ancient rituals together with the Christian ones. The result was a strong resentment toward Christianity, and the Chinese refused to cooperate with the Portuguese colonists. The pope's decision thus crippled Portuguese power in the East, which would later lead to some historical events of great importance, such as the rise of the British East India Company and the Opium Wars.

Similar to China, in India, the missionary work was done by Roberto de Nobili, who adopted the Brahmin way of life to make Christianity appear closer to Hinduists. He was an exceptional linguist, and he used his skills to write the psalms and catechism in the Sanskrit, Telugu, and Tamil languages. It is possible that Catholicism didn't take root in the Far East because it was strongly connected to colonialism. The natives were not inclined to trust the foreigners, as they often exploited them as a cheap workforce or even enslaved them. It certainly didn't help that the pope established the papal Congregatio de Propaganda Fide (Congregation for the Evangelization of Peoples) in 1622, by which all missionary work was centralized and put under strict papal control. This system also allowed royal patronage, which meant that the European rulers had direct influence over the congregation and were able to use it for their personal political goals.

The renewed Catholic spirit was also the cause for some of the bloodiest wars in European history. Through the works of the Jesuits and other Catholic missionaries, Poland, parts of Germany, France, and the Netherlands returned to Catholicism. But elsewhere, the missionary work was not enough, and many secular rulers implemented the religious cause in their political conflicts. One of the most powerful monarchs of the 16th century was Philip of Spain, who considered himself a zealous champion of Catholicism. He did everything that was in his power to restore papal authority over the whole of Europe. In 1588, he launched his whole armada against England. Though his motive was mainly political, he also strove to bring this island kingdom back under papal guidance. Queen Elizabeth used all her power to defend her nation, and she used her political power for her country to remain Protestant.

In France, a series of bloody conflicts between Catholics and Huguenots raged between 1562 and 1598, and they are remembered as the Wars of Religion. The end came when Protestant King Henry IV finally accepted Catholicism in his Edict of Nantes. However, he decreed that there would be freedom of religion for his subjects and did not force them to convert to one religion or the other. Sweden almost returned to the Catholic faith with King Sigismund, who was very obedient to Rome. But his Protestant uncle, Charles, defeated him before he could impose Catholicism on his kingdom. In 1598, he was forced into exile, together with the Jesuits, who were his allies.

The last and probably most gruesome and destructive religious war was fought in Germany. This was none other than the Thirty Years' War (1618-1648). It started when the Tridentine reform of the church resulted in the rise of Catholicism. To prevent the election of a Protestant emperor, the Habsburgs worked on replacing the Elector Palatinate with a Catholic one. When they succeeded, the mostly Protestant nobility of the Palatinate revolted. The result was a war that combined both religious affairs and European politics. Soon almost all of Europe was fighting.

During the first phase of the war, Holy Roman Emperor Ferdinand II of the Austrian House of Habsburg was victorious. He almost succeeded in bringing the whole of Germany back to the papacy. But King Gustav II Adolph of Sweden felt obliged to intervene. He was a Protestant, and he held some territories within the Holy Roman Empire. However, in 1631, he allied himself with Cardinal Richelieu of France, proving that the political goals of the secular leaders were more important than the religious ones. The Thirty Years' War ended with the Treaty of Westphalia, by which the Catholics and Protestants gained equal rights under German law.

At this point, it became very clear that the Christian unity in Europe was gone forever. Moreover, the Catholic Church had lost its authority over the European faith, as some of the most powerful and influential countries, such as England, Sweden, and Prussia, were purely Protestant. However, the Council of Trent and the reforms that followed set the Catholic Church on a strong course into the future. In the 17th century, the church became a strong and very spiritual institution with enormous self-confidence. The popes were once more in complete control of the church, and this time, they were willing to implement the reforms on all levels. The result was the regained capability to meet the religious needs of the Catholic population. Although followers had been lost in Europe, the church replaced them with new followers overseas. The Catholics started gaining victories on all fronts: spiritual, missionary, intellectual, and cultural.

Chapter 12 – The Enlightened Thought in the Catholic Church

Cornelius Jansen by Evêque d'Ypres,
https://en.wikipedia.org/wiki/Cornelius_Jansen#/media/File:Cornelius_Jansen,_Ev%C3%A
Aque_d'Ypres_(1585-1638).png

The Catholic elán for the reformation of the church came to a halt by the middle of the 17th century. But this time, the change wasn't religious. Throughout Europe, intellectual and cultural thought shifted from a Christian viewpoint to a secular one. The intellectual minds of Europe, some of them not even belonging to any religion, sketched a new worldview that would come to dominate Western civilization for the centuries to come. Those who participated in the new intellectual and cultural movement, known as the Enlightenment, took away the knowledge that was in the hands of the church and offered an alternative in regards to the universe, human nature, civilization and society, science, and even religion. The world they created was free of ecclesiastical control, which allowed the secular culture to rise. The main principles of the Enlightenment came from social experience and reason, not the Gospels and the church as an institution.

The Catholic Church, with its roots deep in tradition, resisted the change and took a defensive stance against modernity. It was unable to develop its religious thought any further and meet the secular thinkers on common ground. Instead, the church resorted to condemning and repressing the new ideas. The result of the Enlightenment was a permanent divorce of secular and religious thought, of secular culture and the church. This divorce has lasted to modern times.

The Origin of the Enlightenment

The new intellectual thought in Europe started with Copernicus and his understanding of the cosmos. He rejected the idea of Earth being the center of the universe, a thought that dominated the medieval period. Rather, he believed in heliocentrism, in which the sun was the center of the universe. This new way of thinking about the cosmos sprouted a myriad of scientists, such as Newton, Galileo, and Kepler, who reshaped our understanding of the physical universe that surrounds us. But the church found this all very threatening. It rejected the philosophy of Aristotle, which conveniently followed the religious teachings of the church through the works of Thomas Aquinas. Even the works of Aristotle posed a threat to church doctrine, but Aquinas was very creative, and he managed to reconcile the truths of science and religion. But this time, such a reconciliation was impossible, as great minds such as Galileo refused to believe that God would want them to keep knowledge a secret. In return, the church condemned Galileo for his view that the earth revolves around the sun.

Critical rationalism was the favorite method used by the Enlightenment thinkers, which only gave the church another excuse to condemn them. René Descartes (1596-1650) first applied mathematical methods in philosophy. He implemented radical doubt as to the method that would reveal the absolute truth. The same method was used by 17th-century scientists, who questioned everything until they could establish a truth that was beyond any possible doubt. But Descartes never used this method to question the truths of the faith. However, his followers did, and soon, every aspect of Catholicism was doubted and exposed to questioning. The church was the primary target of the new critical thinkers because its traditionalism was regarded as the epitome of prejudices. The leader of the rationalists who dared to attack church dogma was Pierre Bayle (1647-1706). He focused his criticism on the matters of religion and questioned its historical foundation.

Another practitioner of biblical criticism was French Oratorian priest Richard Simon (1638-1712), who tried to convince the church that not all criticism was bad. He insisted on the critical study of the Bible as if it was just another historical document. He questioned the authorship of the Gospels, but he argued that the Catholic understanding of the tradition was valid. Nevertheless, the church authorities were alarmed by his work and called for its suppression. The church missed another great opportunity to adapt its ideas to the modern way of thinking. In the church's view, the Scripture could be interpreted only by following the tradition, which means that the Scripture could only be understood in the way the fathers of the church promulgated.

Another point of conflict between Enlightenment thought and Catholic tradition was the understanding of the concept of religious freedom. Both Catholics and Protestants saw Christian unity as the only successful basis of the social order. But the idea of the Enlightenment was that each individual was free to worship as they saw fit. The Catholic and Protestant leaders couldn't accept this idea and thought that every country had to have an established church around which society would be structured. Even those countries that implemented freedom of religious choice in their laws couldn't accept this radical new way of defining freedom. For them, the choice was between Catholicism and Protestantism, and no individual was free to set their personal religious views as the basis of worship.

However, the Enlightenment philosophers were determined to fight for complete religious freedom. Their main argument was the personal nature of faith and the fact that religious truth could not be subjected to objective proof. They regarded coercion as the ultimate evil since it left no room for personal choice. These philosophers also believed in personal autonomy. This means they could reject the truth that was forced upon them by authority figures and accept only those truths that could be proven with empirical and rational methods. The church had no sympathy for the ideas of freedom and autonomy. To claim them was heresy. The centralized Roman Church found it very easy to effectively suppress the heresy of the Enlightened philosophers, and because of this, Catholicism became the bastion of intolerance and bigotry.

The Religion of Humanity and Progress

Optimism was one of the main traits of the Enlightenment and probably the main reason it was so attractive and successful. The question of original sin was a subject of bitter disagreement between the Catholic leaders and the philosophers of the 17th century. While the church regarded it as a source of human evil and wickedness, the Enlightenment thinkers claimed people were born good and that it was their use of reason that assured them happiness. Connected with this thought was the issue of progress. When asked if humanity is heading for the "golden age," the church had a very simple answer: No. The Enlightenment philosophers claimed yes. The church's stance has its origin in tradition, which dictates that humans had their golden age in the idyllic past and are now awaiting the Final Judgment. The philosophers, on the other hand, looked at the scientific progress happening all around them and claimed that life was only going to get better. Real material progress was observable in the new better roads, safer conduct of business, accumulated wealth, comfortable homes, sturdier ships, development of optics, the invention of calculating machines, and so on. The Enlightenment thinkers believed that if men could shake off the archaic institutions that imposed fanaticism and dogmatism on humanity, a new level of happiness could be reached.

This new idea of humanity and progress was even observed as a new religion, and its most fervent apostle was Marquis de Condorcet (1743-1794). He sketched a universal history, and in it, the earth was a place where paradise, equivalent to the Christian heaven, could be achieved. He called this paradise the tenth epoch, a period in which superstition would be forgotten, crime would be inexistent, and wars would be forgotten. He claimed that ignorance was the source of all evil and that only the progress of science and society could overcome it. De Condorcet embodied the ideas of the Enlightenment in his brave thought that all humans should have the same rights, regardless of their sex or race. But his thinking was too advanced, and for his efforts to bring a constitutional government to France, he was arrested. He died in prison.

The preachers of this new secular faith started questioning some of the most sacred tenets of Christianity. The nature of man, individual conscience, the purpose of life, and the source of evil were some of the main themes they debated. They invented a type of religion, Deism, which based one's belief in God solely on rational thought. It was upon its followers to strike at the very center of the Christian religion. And in the 17th century, they did so by questioning the revelation. They thought the revelation was unnecessary, as religion should be "natural," which for them meant reasonable, simple, and just enough to satisfy the spiritual needs of humanity. They also thought that the order of the universe and its simple existence were proof enough that God existed. Their religion is defined as rational theism, and they practiced it with strict criticism of the Bible.

Deism had its origin in England, long before the time in which Marquis de Condorcet lived. It was first conceived by Lord Herbert of Cherbury (1583–1648), who thought that "natural" religion would end the discord among the Christian sects. Lord Cherbury had many followers who developed the ideas of Deism and wrote a significant number of essays on the topics of religious belief. Deist ideas even penetrated the church, and some priests played with the idea of combining Catholic and Deist thoughts.

Deism reached its peak in France, where the struggle between the new faith and the old church started. The famous French philosopher Voltaire was a Deist, and he set on a path of battling the Christian Church, all in the name of the Enlightenment. He savagely attacked the dogma, ethics, traditions, and history of the church. His anti-Christian epos concluded with the *Dictionnaire philosophique* (*Philosophical Dictionary*), which was published in 1764. This book was met with such disgust that in the Netherlands, Spain, Rome, and Geneva, it was publicly burned. The French Catholics were never able to produce an individual who would be able to meet Voltaire in debate as an equal. At one point, the Jesuits seemed as if they would be able to lead the church into a positive relationship with the thinkers of the Enlightenment, but they were suppressed in 1763, and all hopes of reconciliation ended.

The fight between the Deists and the Catholics in France escalated even more in 1752 when Sorbonne University published a thesis, which was authored by Jean-Martin de Prades (also known as Abbé de Prades). The thesis he presented was supposed to defend the concept of revelation in Christianity. However, his thesis was heavily influenced by the ideas of French philosopher Diderot, a prominent figure of the Enlightenment. The thesis turned out to be an open attack on church dogma. Suddenly, it became clear that even Sorbonne had succumbed to a rational way of thinking. The incident divided the public of France into two camps, those who followed the Enlightenment and those who supported the Christians. Their struggle continued for several more decades before it was interrupted by the French Revolution (1789-1799).

The Internal Strife of the Catholic Church

The church started losing its ground in the fight against the Enlightenment during the 17th and 18th centuries. It also suffered internal separatism between Jansenism and Gallicanism. These two factions were the cause of many significant controversies that weakened the church. Perhaps it was this internal struggle that prevented the church from mounting a full defense against the free thinkers, which would ultimately lead to its failure.

Jansenism started with the bishop of Ypres, who was also a professor at Louvain University. His name was Cornelius Jansen (1585-1638), and he wrote a book titled *Augustinus*, which was published only after his death. In this book, Jansen appealed to the authority of Saint Augustine while trying to explain the nature of original sin, God's grace, and the free will of humans. He believed human nature was radically corrupted, which his opponents considered too close to Calvinist thinking. After his death, his followers expanded on his ideas, which attracted the attention of the pope, who assigned a commission that would examine their five cardinal doctrines. Finally, Pope Innocent X condemned Jansenism in 1653, declaring its denial of free will in the acceptance of grace as being heretical. This means that while Catholic doctrine thought that it was up to humans and their free will to accept or refuse God's grace, Jansenism preached God loved humanity and would grace them regardless of their acceptance or refusal.

This didn't stop Jansen's followers. They found a new leader in Antoine Arnauld (1612–1694), and they established their headquarters in the abbey of Port-Royal-des-Champs, France. One of the most profound followers of Jansenism was a famous French inventor and mathematician, Blaise Pascal. In 1656/57, he wrote his famous satire, the *Provincial Letters*, in which he attacked the most bitter enemies of Jansenism, the Jesuits. At its core, the Jansenist philosophy was very pessimistic. They believed that God would bestow his grace only on a few chosen ones. The rest of humanity was condemned to forever suffer for their sins. And sinful they were because the Jansenists believed that the original sin corrupted the people's souls. Everything one did was sinful; even one's virtues were nothing more than vices in disguise. Jesuits, on the other hand, were more optimistic and closer to the thinking of the Enlightenment. They believed that even without God's grace, a man could live a life of virtue and observe the moral righteousness of his free will. Since the main aim of the church was to embrace all men, they naturally supported the views of the Jesuits and condemned the Jansenists.

King Louis XIV joined the popes in the persecution of the Jansenists, whose ideas managed to spread throughout the ranks of the French clergy. In 1695, a Jansenist named Louis Antoine de Noailles was elevated to the position of archbishop of Paris. But the king drove out the nuns from their abbey of Port-Royal-des-Champs, and by 1760, almost none of the bishops showed leniency to the Jansenists. Soon, they became a very small and insignificant sect, but they never formally broke off from the Catholic Church.

Another movement that stirred unrest in the Catholic Church was Gallicanism. The followers of this sect wanted to restrict papal interference in the affairs of national churches and to decrease papal influence over the secular rulers. According to the Gallicans, bishops needed more independence and a break from the papacy's constant control. On a theological level, they denied papal infallibility since they believed infallibility belonged to the church as a whole. This means that all the decrees a pope or an ecclesiastical council would issue needed revision and acceptance of the universal ecclesiastical episcopate.

The Gallicans originated in France, but their work wasn't confined only to one country. In fact, their ideas seeped into the governments of many western European countries that wanted to restrict the church and turn it into a state department. The Church of England, the Lutheran Church in Germany and Scandinavia, and the Catholic ones in France and the Habsburg Empire would all become unified with the state, and they would be reduced to a junior partner in this union. Some monarchs eventually managed to take control over the national churches, but less so in the Catholic states, as the Roman See was far away in Italy. But even in France and the Habsburg Empire, rulers gained the right to appoint the bishops and to prevent papal decrees from being published. Pressured by the secular rulers, universities and seminars started teaching Gallicanism, which dominated church-state relations in the 18th century. And for the next two centuries, the papacy would be unable to confront and defeat it. That would happen only during the First Vatican Council in the 19th century.

In Germany, Gallicanism took another form and name: Febronianism. The name of this religious movement comes from its founder Nicholas von Hontheim (1701–1790), who published his work under the pseudonym Febronius. His tract *On the State of the Church and the Legitimate Power of the Roman Pontiff* (published in 1763) supported the Gallicans' theory that a general council should have authority over the pope. He also denied the separate infallibility of the pope and claimed the divine right for the bishops. But Febronianism went further than Gallicanism with its reformation program, which had the unity of all Christians as its main goal.

When the pope condemned Febronianism, sixteen out of twenty-six German bishops refused to publish the condemnation. Even the archbishop of Trier was unwilling to support it. But Hontheim himself submitted to the pope, not wanting to stir the discord within the church. The archbishops of Mainz, Trier, and Salzburg then met, and together, they proclaimed episcopal independence from Rome. This was a clear sign that Febronianism continued to develop within Germany. However, the archbishops failed to rally the bishops to their cause. Nevertheless, the movement continued to mature in Germany, and it was only put out during the First Vatican Council, at the same time when Gallicanism was canceled.

The Catholic Church reached the lowest point of its prestige and influence during the 18th century. Its inability to tackle the Enlightenment thinkers and scientists, its suppression of the Jesuits, and its failed efforts to counter the works of the Jansenists and Gallicans are only some of the manifestations of the popes' weak leadership. One of the main reasons for the church's dismal state was the alienation of the throne and altar. The church became subjected to the government, as secular rulers gained power over the popes and their decisions. Their ability to veto papal elections secured the pontificates of some of the weakest popes the Catholic Church had seen since the fall of Constantinople. But the dislodgement of the church out of the traditions it had followed for so very long resulted in social, cultural, and political disruptions.

Chapter 13 – The French Revolution and the End of the Old Order

The arrest of Pope Pius VII by the French in 1809 by Benoit Lhoest.
Benoit Lhoest, CC BY-SA 3.0 <https://creativecommons.org/licenses/by-sa/3.0>, via
Wikimedia Commons
https://commons.wikimedia.org/wiki/File:Pie_VII_Arrestation_par_le_G%C3%A9n%C3%
A9ral_Radet.png

Although the churches, both Catholic and Protestant, lost their power during the 17th and 18th centuries, they were deeply embedded in the lives of the people, and they were an integral part of society. They were established as official national religions, and their institutions and clergy enjoyed the prestige and prerogatives bestowed upon them by their governments. The religious leaders were considered aristocracy, and they spent their lives accordingly. The union of the state and the church was an old concept, and it seemed as if it would continue to exist for centuries to come. But revolution exploded in France and expanded throughout Europe, and churches everywhere felt the consequences.

The French Church was the first to feel the impact of the revolution. The traditional dominant position it had in society was completely shattered, and the church never managed to regain it again. Catholic churches across Europe shared a similar fate in the subsequent years, but the Protestant churches were not as severely affected, at least not in the beginning. However, the revolution sprouted out of liberalism and democracy, forces that would eventually disrupt all the churches of western Europe.

The Origins of the French Revolution

The French Revolution is considered the climax of the Enlightenment. It began as an experiment in reforming the French government, and it didn't have a violent character at the beginning. The king called on 1,200 selected deputies from all corners of France to meet at Versailles and solve the financial crisis in the spring of 1789. Half of the gathered deputies decided that France needed a radical reform of its government that the king couldn't provide. Their goal was to replace the existing regime with a society that would be built on the economic ideas of the Enlightenment. This meant giving the middle class political power and abolishing the privileges and prerogatives the aristocracy gained by birth. They also advocated complete economic freedom that would be free of all forms of control. This would mean that everyone would be able to enjoy their private properties. They wanted to build a humane society that would be efficient and orderly.

The deputies decided that France would no longer be ruled solely by a monarch who had the divine right. Instead, a monarch would share his rule with a council of elected representatives from all over the country. The king and his supporters, namely the aristocracy, resisted this proposal. But the Third Estate (composed of the commoners) was determined, and when King Louis XVI ordered them to disband, they defied him. At that point, Louis was unable to use force against his people, and he decided to capitulate and allow the formation of the National Assembly.

However, the king didn't give up. He brought mercenaries to France and used them to reestablish his absolute power. The people responded by forming their own army, the National Guard. People all over France gave their support to the revolution, and the king had no other choice but to submit. But now, the nation was too angry, and they wouldn't allow Louis XVI to come back as a monarch, not even if he was to work with the National Assembly. His constant efforts to work against the revolutionaries finally resulted in his execution in 1792 and the formation of the French Republic.

The Catholic Church was the only allowed Christian religion in France at the time, and it was an integral part of the old regime and order. The French clergy was always picked from the ranks of the nobility, and they were the members of the First Estate. This meant they held privileged positions, and they used their power to control education and public relief. The church was the only institution that registered marriages, births, and deaths, and it also used censorship whenever a publication would be suspected of harming the nation's faith and morals. There were some initiatives made to organize a reform of the church, but they were small and never powerful enough. The church had a strong hold over the majority of the people.

The Church and the Revolution

At first, the church supported the revolution. Perhaps the clergy realized early on that the majority of the Frenchmen were revolutionists. It even joined the Third Estate in voting against the absolute monarchy. The clergy went so far in their support of the National Assembly that they willingly handed over their privileges and agreed to the confiscation of church properties. After all, this measure would save France's economy. The people were thrilled that the church was on their side, and the laymen of the National Assembly showed no animosity toward the church. They agreed to recognize Catholicism as the official religion of the nation. However, they also gave freedom of religion to the Protestants and the Jews. The Catholic Church was against this, but it had no other choice but to submit.

But soon enough, a schism between the church and the laymen occurred, as the National Assembly took it upon itself to reform the church. They issued the Civil Constitution of the Clergy, and with it, they abolished the collection of tithes, reduced the number of bishops, and established administrative units for each diocese. They also wanted the French citizens to elect the bishops instead of the clergy and have the state pay their wages. This constitution meant that the pope would no longer have any control over the French Church, as it would be nationalized. The Catholics were outraged, and the majority of them abandoned the revolution.

The National Assembly pressed hard on the clergy to accept the oath to the constitution, but the clergy first appealed to the pope for advice. Pope Pius VI was an absolute monarch, and in 1791, he responded by condemning the Constitution of the Clergy, forbidding the French bishops and priests to take the oath. However, it took him eight months to reach this decision, and in that time, the National Assembly had already forced the clergy to accept the oath or abandon their office. Only seven bishops accepted the oath, as well as around half of the clergy. The rest decided not to give in. Although the majority of the bishops and lower clergy supported the revolution and agreed that reform of the church was needed, their primary allegiance was with the church. They felt that if they accepted the oath, they would endanger the spiritual sovereignty of the Catholic Church.

The schism between the National Assembly and the church also resulted in the split of the Catholic community into two factions: those who accepted the oath and those who remained loyal to Rome. Those who refused the constitution were expelled from their parishes and churches, and soon, they were also accused of disloyalty to the revolutionary cause. They were blamed as much as the aristocracy. The papal legates did nothing to help the clergy in France, although they preached counterrevolution to the French refugees in Germany. The clergy that refused to take the oath experienced outright persecution once Austria and Prussia decided to invade France and put down the revolution. The French nationalists accused these priests and bishops of being traitors who worked in allegiance with the foreign monarchies to bring back absolutism in France.

On May 26th, 1792, the National Assembly passed a decree by which they decided to deport all of the nonjuring (those who refused the oath) clergy. Thirty to forty thousand priests were driven away from their hometowns and forced into exile. Some of them chose to stay in France, although they had to remain in hiding. The next year, the death penalty was installed for the clergy that decided to return to France from their exile. The nonjurors who remained in the country started preaching in cellars and barns, providing the loyal Catholics with the Mass in secrecy.

The clergy that supported the constitution had it good at the beginning. They celebrated each victory of the revolutionaries, and they supported the new laws that were passed by the National Assembly. But even though they were loyal to the revolution, the happy relations with the republic didn't last long. With the fall of the monarchy, friction between the church and the state was created. The clergy remained royalist, and they couldn't agree upon the execution of the king. But there was also another reason for the defiance of the clergy. The revolution itself started feeling as if it was a religion. The National Assembly demanded sacred oaths from the people, and sacred trees were included in some of the public ceremonies. The street names in many towns were changed from saints to revolutionary heroes. The people started giving their babies non-Christian names, and church relics were often seized by the state to be melted and dedicated to other purposes. The revolution had quite different values than the church, and the patriots started attacking the clergy for being different.

The French Republic almost abandoned Christianity altogether. The adoption of a calendar in 1793 was just the first step in the dechristianization of the nation. They abandoned the Christian Sunday and a seven-day week. In its place, they installed a ten-day week, and all the Christian holidays were suspended, even Christmas. This new calendar had the purpose of installing the rule of reason above religion. Some ex-priests joined the dechristianization of France and started denouncing religious sophistry. They claimed their churches were turned into temples of reason, and they started mocking the Catholic liturgy. They also pressured the clergy to marry and have children so they could join the nation in producing a new generation of patriots. In Paris, all the churches were closed, and the city bishop was forced to resign. In Notre Dame, the Cult of Reason was celebrated, and during the ceremony, an actress was crowned on the altar as the Goddess of Reason.

Many cults sprouted and tried to replace Catholicism. Among them were Deism, Robespierre's Cult of the Supreme Being, and Theophilantropy, the latter of which came the closest to becoming a new national religion. However, none of them managed to survive for long. A large part of the populace was illiterate and found the new ceremonies too abstract, and they couldn't relate to them. The new religions simply faded away, as no one was willing to support them. By 1794, the dechristianization of France had seemed to pass, and the next year, the National Assembly passed a decree by which religious freedom was guaranteed for everyone. This meant people were free to choose their religion, and the people rushed to re-open the Catholic churches.

The Revolution and the Pope

Although the Catholic Church in France was reviving, the revolutionists didn't rest. This time, they attacked the pope. In 1796, Napoleon Bonaparte (1769–1821) led a campaign to Italy and occupied Milan. In northern Italy, he started several republics based on the French model. At first, he had no intentions of attacking Rome, and he even recognized the pope's sovereignty over the Papal States. But when a French general was murdered by a corporal of the pontificate guard, Napoleon entered Rome. Pope Pius VI was arrested, and many treasures of the Vatican were confiscated and shipped to the Louvre in Paris. Suspecting that the Austrians would try to rescue the pope, he was taken to France. But Pius was already old, and the journey proved to be too difficult for him. He died at Valence at the age of eighty-one.

Because of the great instability in Rome, the election of the next pope was opened only in 1799 in Venice under the protection of the Austrian emperor. The new pope elected, Pius VII, was a compromise, as he was a Benedictine bishop of Imola, a northern Italian city that was turned into a republic by Napoleon. The new pope soon proved his worth, as he had all the necessary characteristics to solve the crisis of the church. By the time Pius VII was elected, Napoleon had defeated the Austrians in Italy and proclaimed himself their master. The future of the church was now in his hands, and luckily, he intended to make peace with Rome. But he was aware that the Catholic Church had a great influence on the French, and he needed to make sure his influence was stronger.

He was aware that dechristianization had failed and that the attempt left a deep wound in the French clergy, which was now divided. Napoleon planned to win over the nonjurors, as they were numerous and more influential than the constitutionalists. But he needed the pope's help if he was to convince the nonjurors to accept the constitution.

In 1801, Napoleon and Pius VII signed a concordat, an agreement between the Holy See and a sovereign state that defines their relationship. The Catholic Church was now officially recognized as the majority religion of France. The concordat ended the schism between the constitutionalists and nonjurors, and Napoleon was celebrated as the only person able to solve the religious problem, which had lasted since the start of the revolution. The concordat had five main points: all the bishops had to resign; the first consul of the republic had the power to appoint the bishops, whom the pope would institute canonically; the church would give up their confiscated properties; the clergy would be paid a salary by the state; and the Catholic religion had to subject itself to the police if it was required to maintain public order.

The last point of the concordat was the most important for Napoleon, as he wanted to use it to limit papal influence over the French Church. He then proceeded to attach numerous articles to the concordat to severely limit the communication between the French Church and the Holy See. The pope didn't like Napoleon's arrogance. He was even forced to attend his imperial coronation just so the whole of Europe would see how the pope, who condemned the revolution, finally succumbed to it and bestowed his blessing on its product, the French Empire.

But Bonaparte soon realized he didn't have strong control over the pope. Pius VII refused to join France in mounting an economic blockade of England because he wanted the Papal States to remain neutral. In turn, Napoleon seized the Papal States, but Pius excommunicated him. The French emperor had the pope arrested in 1808 and brought to France, where he stayed for the next six years. The pope displayed an enormous will to endure, and he spent his days in confinement praying and meditating. He also refused to institute the new bishops, and by 1814, many French dioceses were vacant. Napoleon lost against the Russians that same year, and he finally realized it was necessary to restore the pope to Rome. Pius VII entered the city on May 24th, 1814, victorious.

The Lingering Effects of the Revolution

With the Congress of Vienna (1814/15), peace was achieved in Europe, and the old Bourbon dynasty was restored to the throne of France. Napoleon was imprisoned on the island of Saint Helena, off the west coast of Africa, where he spent his last days. The pope was restored as the absolute monarch of the Papal States. However, the effects of the revolution remained visible, as the social and political transformation of France was too vast. France couldn't return to the old order, where a monarch was determined by birth and where they ruled by divine right. Religious life had also changed. Although the people remained mainly Catholic, the effects of dechristianization could be seen in the anti-clericalism that remained. The process of secularization that started with the revolution couldn't be stopped. The most visible expressions of secularization were civil marriage, divorce, and secular schools that opened across the country.

The French Revolution could be felt in the churches of other nations too. The biggest change happened in Germany, where the Catholic prince bishops lost their feudal possessions. Protestant rulers rose to power, although their subjects were mostly Catholic. Church properties were confiscated, and monasteries were disbanded. The clergy and the school were paid by the state, which reduced the church to the position of a governmental subordinate.

Interestingly enough, the papacy benefited from the French Revolution. Pius VII improved the image of the papal office with his heroic endurance in France, and he proved that a pope could have settled the fate of the church if one had been willing to make a compromise with a secular ruler. But not all benefices were installed by the pope's actions. In fact, the French Revolution freed the church by shattering the monarchy it used to serve. There were no more enlightened rulers who installed their people in the offices of the church. The old order ended, and the popes were now free to rebuild Rome as the vital center of Catholicism. The church was finally free to return to its original spiritual mission.

Chapter 14 – Liberal Catholics

Christogram used by the Jesuit order.
https://en.wikipedia.org/wiki/Society_of_Jesus#/media/File:Ihs-logo.svg

The early 19th century birthed some of the greatest thinkers who were committed to reviving the church. They were liberal Catholics, and they were optimistic about the direction the world was going after the revolution. They wanted to reform the church in such a way that it would build a new positive relationship with secular society and culture. Liberal Christians wanted a church that would support constitutional freedoms, which included the freedom of religion. But their ideas were quickly condemned by Pope Gregory XVI. But his successor, Pius IX, had a reputation for being very liberal. The liberal Catholic movement was revitalized during his pontificate, but Pius proved not to be what they imagined.

When Pius IX refused to liberate the Papal States, everyone in Europe understood they had no chance of finding a common language with the pope. However, the Papal States had no military power that could match the people's will to liberate themselves. The pope had no other choice but to turn to spiritual weapons he could wield against his subjects. In his *Syllabus of Errors* (issued in 1864), Pius condemned liberalism. The church hardened toward the pleas of the liberal Catholics and secular society.

The Catholic Revival and the Political Liberalism

After the French Revolution and the fall of Napoleon Bonaparte, the Catholic Church underwent a spiritual and intellectual renaissance. It became, once again, the central religious institution, and it had a powerful influence on public affairs. Pope Pius VII was celebrated as a hero across the whole of Europe for refusing to submit to Napoleon. The moral authority of the papacy was restored, and Ercole Consalvi, Cardinal Secretary of the Papal States, easily persuaded the Congress of Vienna to return the Papal States to the pope's control.

In 1814, the Jesuit order was reestablished as if to mark the revival of the Catholic Church. The popularity of this religious order grew, and soon, they numbered thousands of members across Europe. New religious orders sprouted, such as the Society of the

Sacred Heart. Catholic schools reopened, and the seminars were once again filled with people eager to debate religious issues. The churches were crowded during the Mass. In 1815, the Society of the Foreign Mission was reestablished, and it worked closely with the Jesuits to rekindle the missionary spirit and take the faith across the world.

But the Catholic revival wasn't only spiritual and moral. There was also an intellectual side to it. Although many European philosophers rejected the skepticism and rationalism of the Enlightenment, they continued to wonder about human nature, the origin of evil, and God's grace. The definitions set by the rational thinkers suddenly felt superficial, and the philosophers of the 19th century felt there was more to the universe than the cold mechanical calculations of the Enlightenment thinkers. It was natural for them to ask for something divine after the bloody revolution and Napoleon's wars. Progress was now seen as the bringer of evil, as human nature wasn't simply good. They needed faith, mystery, and tradition. It was only natural to return to the Catholic Church, which was, in its nature, conservative and traditional. The sentiment didn't only lead them back to the church but also to political reaction and cultural romanticism. Once again, the great minds of Europe saw the ideal of human existence in the idolized past. Thinkers such as German Friedrich von Schlegel (1772–1829) thought that tradition was a way of slowly evolving and progressing. He thought of the now past Holy Roman Empire as an ideal of political and religious unity, and he dared to dream of a Europe unified under the regency of the pope.

During this revival of the Catholic Church, one question remained unanswered: How is Catholicism going to relate itself to liberalism? As a new political movement, liberalism continued the ideas of the Enlightenment and the French Revolution. It was one of those very complicated questions that would once again divide the Catholic Church.

The supporters of the newly established liberalism movement were mainly from the middle and professional classes. They wanted a written constitution and a parliamentary political system that would guarantee personal rights. They were the continuation of rational thinking, and they were secularists. Liberals believed a church shouldn't decide on matters such as education and marriage. As a result, the liberals did not have much support from the Catholics and none from the clergy.

The period after Napoleon's wars was a trial for the liberals. The Congress of Vienna restored the monarchs' power, who then surrounded themselves with conservative statesmen eager to keep their kings on the throne. One such statesman was Austrian Minister Klemens von Metternich, who worked hard on keeping the spirit of the French Revolution dead. He saw enemies of the state on every corner, and he fought the liberals and radical students with the use of secret police, censorship of publications, and personal watchdogs positioned at universities and governmental institutions.

The liberal cause seemed hopeless, as men like Metternich were installed everywhere. Only the Prussian king gave thought to a constitution for his people, but he quickly abandoned the idea when Metternich pressured European rulers to issue Carlsbad Decrees. With these decrees, the secret police were given more freedom, and they were able to assert strict control of universities. Liberals and radical thinkers were forced underground. In Spain, King Ferdinand VII arrested liberals and reestablished the inquisition. In France, King Louis XVIII tried to remain neutral by pleasing both the right and left. But his successor, Charles X, had no choice but to lean toward the right because political strife made it impossible to remain neutral. In England, British Parliament passed the Six Acts in 1819, which were designed to keep radical ideas in check.

The Catholic Church decided to side with the monarchs against liberal thought. Many religious orders played a role in suppressing revolutionary ideas, such as the Methodists in England. In Poland, Belgium, Ireland, and France, the Catholic clergy preached obedience to the state and the established order of monarchies. They burned the works of notable rationalists such as Voltaire and asked their followers to swear an oath of loyalty to the church and their ruler. In Italy, with the death of Pope Pius VII in 1823, the Catholic reactionists took control over the Papal States. They dismissed all of the institutions established by Napoleon, such as law courts, and they immediately stopped the vaccination program. Priests were put in all of the secular offices of the Papal States, and the Jews were put into ghettos. Soon enough, an alliance with the monarch among many European nation-states resulted in a position of privilege in the Catholic Church. The primary and elementary schools were returned to the church's control but not secular universities, although the clergy tried to abolish them.

Liberal Catholicism

Not all of the clergy was in an alliance with the rulers and conservative nobles. Those who were far away from such alliances allowed liberal ideas to seep into their churches and started their own movement, liberal Catholicism. Its founder was a French priest named Félicité de Lamennais (1782–1854), who had inclinations toward the prophetic role. He displayed an astonishing ability to predict how the future of Europe and Christianity would look like. As a youth, Lamennais was enthralled by the Enlightenment, and he exercised his free thought. But eventually, his brother convinced him of the wonders of faith, and Lamennais was ordained in 1817. He proved to be a very pious priest, and he worked hard on reviving Catholicism in France. However, his indulgence in the Enlightenment made him cautious of the social, political, and cultural changes the French Revolution brought, and he had a vision of a Catholic Church with a different role to play in modern society. His visions and ideas are why he was labeled radical and a founder of liberal Catholicism.

The first and main idea Lamennais had regarding the church was its complete separation from the state. He regarded this separation as throwing off the chains with which the church was bound to the monarchy. Only by doing this would the Catholic Church gain the freedom it needed to reform itself and become relevant to modern society. But Lamennais also predicted the doom of the reactionary monarchy and wanted the church to stay out of it and survive. He wanted a strong papacy that would have supreme authority over both the spiritual and political scenes of Catholic states. For this, he was considered the founder of 19th-century ultramontanism (a belief in strong papal authority).

Lamennais claimed the separation of the church and state would also mean the liberalization of education because only that would ensure religious freedom and the freedom of thought. Furthermore, he advocated the freedom of the press because censorship could not be trusted. Finally, this visionary surpassed the political thought of his period and imagined a complete democracy where universal suffrage would be the norm. He claimed that only if everyone had the power to decide could complete freedom be attained. He wanted the church to stop relying on the monarchs and start trusting the people.

The ideas of Félicité de Lamennais attracted the young clergy and educated Catholic laymen. They helped him start *L'Avenir* (*The Future*), a daily newspaper that had "God and Freedom" as its main slogan. The goal of this daily publication was to educate the people and plant the seeds of Catholic liberalism. However, he met strong opposition with the French bishops, who accused him of undermining the papacy's authority, an order implemented by Jesus Christ himself. The archbishop of Paris condemned the ideas of liberal Catholics, claiming the separation of church and state would bring poverty to the church. Lamennais agreed, but unlike the archbishop, he welcomed the idea of poverty, as it was the church's original state. He further explained that only the priests who suffered poverty could truly relate to the people, especially to the poor, weak, and ill.

But the bishops remained unmoved. They were stubborn in their thought that separation would bring destruction upon the church. They banned *L'Avenir* and doomed it to financial ruin. The publication's audience was already very limited since Catholic liberalism was a young idea. Even liberals were against it, as they were afraid of the democratic spirit it preached. Lamennais then decided to appeal directly to the pope, strongly believing that Catholic liberalism could at least be recognized and legalized. But this was a mistake, as Pope Gregory XVI was completely against liberalism. After all, at that very moment, the pope was trying to subdue the secret revolutionary society, the Carbonari, that terrorized the countryside of the Papal States and assassinated several papal officials.

Lamennais and his supporters reached Rome in 1831 and submitted a very long memorandum to the pope. This memorandum was a survey of the relationship between the state and the church since the return of the Bourbon dynasty to the French throne. Furthermore, Lamennais used the opportunity to point out why the separation was the only reasonable solution for the church's freedom. Lamennais had to wait for the pope's response for weeks, during which time he became aware of the political events in Italy and the persecution of the revolutionists. He began to realize his mission in Rome was futile. Gregory XVI finally sent a response, a bull titled *Mirari vos*, in which he denounced the liberal Christian doctrines and rejected the separation of church and state. The pope also called the freedom of conscience a madness and the freedom of the press an absolute abomination.

At the same time, Catholic liberalism in Belgium won a great victory. There, the Catholics joined the liberals in their fight against the Dutch rule, and in 1830, they managed to overthrow the Dutch king with a revolution. The next year, the Belgian constitution was drawn up through the joint efforts of liberals and Catholics. The basis of this constitution was the same freedoms that the pope denounced in *Mirari vos*. After Belgium, other countries started taking up the revolutionary spirit. In Britain, the Great Reform Act was passed in 1832, by which liberals gained the power to share the government with conservatives. In central Europe, conservatism still remained in full control. Lamennais exchanged several letters with the pope, and after some persuasion and fear for his soul, he defected from Catholic liberalism. But his followers continued the struggle, now under the leadership of Charles Forbes René de Montalembert, who immediately started a Catholic political party in France. This was the first such party in Europe.

The Revolutions of 1848 was an important turning point for the liberals. They were incredibly successful in western Europe, and they inspired the people of central and southern Europe to demand a constitution from their monarchs. Metternich was forced out of Vienna, although the Habsburg ruler managed to suppress the revolution in Austria, Hungary, and Italy. The Prussian king was briefly dethroned, but he quickly managed to return to power. Nevertheless, liberal ideas remained popular among the people, and they were even promoted by Romanticism, a cultural movement.

When Pius IX (papacy 1846–1878) was elected as pope, the liberal Catholics saw a glimmer of hope. This pope was open to liberal ideas, at least at first. He released political prisoners, started sharing the government of the Papal States with laymen, abolished press censorship, and issued a constitution to his people, although he preserved his absolute power by giving himself the right to veto the elections of the bicameral parliament. The changes Pius IX introduced were liberal in nature, but they didn't mean the church was becoming liberal. He never intended to implement the religious freedoms that were the basis of Catholic liberalism. Pope Pius IX was only following the political momentum of his period and had no real intention to move beyond what was necessary and truly change the traditional and conservative stance of the Catholic Church.

The pope's parliament declared war on Austria because it wanted Italian unification, and parts of the peninsula were still under Habsburg rule. But Pius couldn't allow a war against another Catholic state, and he vetoed the parliament. This led to the complete breakdown of the political system he had implemented. The democratic extremists exploded with rage, and the streets of Rome were filled with angry people demonstrating against the papal veto. Pius IX was forced to flee Rome, and the leader of the Italian liberation movement, Giuseppe Garibaldi, entered Rome in 1848, where he set up a democratic republic. But the pope returned two years later, following the French Army, and he regained control over the Papal States. He was resolved to show no more leniency toward liberalism. He proclaimed liberalism equal to anarchy and canceled the constitution.

In the state of Piedmont, the liberals remained in power, and they established some new laws that the church found offensive. They completely secularized education and abolished all religious orders. But the government of Piedmont didn't stop there. Their main idea was to unite the Italian states under their monarchy, and they planned to start with the Papal States. A series of uprisings were organized, and the Piedmont government pretended to move their army to quell the rebellion. Their real intention was to occupy the Papal States. The pope didn't have an army large enough to defend him, and he was defeated in 1860. However, Piedmont allowed the pope to keep control of the city of Rome.

Camillo Cavour, Prime Minister of Piedmont, wanted to achieve peace with the pope, and he offered him independence and exclusive jurisdiction over the church, freedom of religious education, ownership of buildings and monuments that traditionally belonged to the church, and a salary for the papal court, papal college, and all Italian clergy and episcopates. The pope believed the laws of the church were eternal and couldn't be subjected to the laws of the men. However, the real reason behind the refusal was the pope's fear that if liberalism took over, the whole of Italy would be subjected to the freedom of religion, which would mean the uncontrolled spread of heresy. Instead of peace, the pope declared war on secular liberalism in his bull, *Syllabus of Errors*, which was issued on December 8th, 1864.

The Syllabus of Errors

The *Syllabus of Errors* listed eighty errors of modern political thought, including naturalism, rationalism, socialism, and liberal capitalism. But out of all eighty errors, the people were most appalled by the pope's condemnation of the freedom of religion, liberalism, and progress. By this point, liberalism had become a mainstream public opinion, and it is no wonder that the *Syllabus of Errors* caused an explosive reaction. Even the moderate Catholics were shocked to hear the pope condemn natural progress and modernization. The average person who read the papal bull couldn't fully comprehend its context, and many of the errors were misinterpreted. To the people, it seemed as if the pope had just declared war on civilization.

As disaster was looming behind the corner, French Bishop Félix Dupanloup tried to rescue the situation. He immediately wrote a commentary to the *Syllabus of Errors* in which he tried to put the bull in its proper context. A system had been put in place in Piedmont with the sole intent of destroying the papacy. Dupanloup tried to explain to the public that Rome had no intention of condemning the liberal constitutions brought about in Belgium, the United States of America, Latin America, and England. The public decided to believe in the commentary of the bull, and Catholic liberalism was defeated, though not eradicated.

The Catholic liberals lost their momentum, and although they were no longer regarded as heretics, they had to endure a disgraceful retreat underground so they wouldn't attract attention to themselves. They didn't change their opinions and ideas but had to tread carefully in order to avoid full condemnation. However, some of them were not that careful. The archbishop of Paris was a liberal, and he felt the urge to reply to the *Syllabus of Errors*, accusing the pope of condemning the modern principles on which the world was standing. He called the pope to support these principles, as it was his duty to unify liberty and authority. But Pius IX was fervently ultramontane, and he would not give up. Through his long pontificate, he only worked to strengthen the papal authority and even define papal infallibility. His stance on liberalism only hardened over time.

Chapter 15 – First Vatican Council and Social Catholicism

First Vatican Council, depicted by Karl Benzinger in 1873.
https://en.wikipedia.org/wiki/First_Vatican_Council#/media/File:Engraving_of_First_Vatic an_Council.jpg

Pope Pius IX was single-handedly responsible for the strengthening of ultramontanism during the 19th century. It was through his *Syllabus of Errors* that liberalism was defeated and that the church regained its grasp over popular opinion. The pope's supporters in major bishoprics and colleges worked hard on reinforcing ultramontanism and papal infallibility. But opposition still existed, and Pius needed to deal with them once and for all. In 1867, he announced his call for the First Vatican Council, giving the impression that its purpose would be to unite the church against the rationalism of the 19th century. The Gallicans, who were still very powerful in France, chose to work with the liberals against the pope and the supporters of ultramontanism. They hoped for a debate, which they could win, but they feared that Pius IX would use the council only to reaffirm his antiliberal stance and strengthen ultramontanism.

The council didn't have its first session until 1868, and the liberals took the opportunity to try and sway public opinion away from the pope. In 1867, a German theologian named Ignaz von Döllinger published his work, *The Pope and the Council*, in which he tried to show how the papacy usurped power over the church throughout history. Other German intellectuals and liberal bishops joined Döllinger in his criticism of papacy, and they announced they would defy papal infallibility. In France, the Gallican Bishop Henri Maret argued more moderately. He declared that the pope needed the agreement of the episcopate to enjoy complete infallibility.

These debates, which occurred before the actual council was called, notified the public what would be the major points of discussion and to bring papal infallibility forth as the most important point. Another purpose was to define the two opposing parties that would lead the debate during the council: the conservative Catholics, who would reaffirm the *Syllabus of Errors* and who endorsed papal infallibility, and the liberals, who opposed the pope. The pre-council debates also made it clear that the conservative Catholics had the majority. Although the liberals represented only around 20 percent of the council, they came from some of the most important Catholic sees, such as the Austro-Hungarian episcopate. There were also many German, American, and French bishops.

The Council

During the first few weeks, it became clear that the pope called the council only to have his infallibility accepted by acclamation instead of by vote. The liberals were annoyed that the pope himself drew up the rules of the council, which was contrary to the rules established at the Council of Trent in 1563. By doing so, the pope restricted the liberals' freedom of initiative. One of the council rules was that only the pope could propose questions to the council. Another was the place where the council would take place, St. Peter's Basilica, which had very bad acoustics. The liberals claimed Pius IX chose this basilica on purpose so that not everyone could hear what was being discussed. Therefore, the liberals would be unable to file complaints. But the greatest concern was that the liberals had no representation in the key committee, which would be responsible for drafting the statement of papal infallibility.

The council started its session in an overwhelming atmosphere of resentment and bitterness. Nevertheless, the bishops started drafting the first document submitted by the pope: his statement on the errors of rationalism, which he considered to be opposed to the Christian religion. During the session, the majority of bishops approved a modification of the council rules that would allow a motion of cloture (quickly ending a debate) even if only ten bishops requested it. They also decided that any motion could be carried if it was voted in by the majority. The previous tradition demanded moral unanimity, and many of the liberal bishops seriously considered abandoning the council and challenging its legitimacy.

When the time came to draft a constitution on the nature of the church, 380 bishops requested to put papal infallibility immediately up for discussion, saying the rest of the draft could be discussed later. The issue was opened on March 6th, 1869, and the agitation began. The opposing parties strove to win over the undecided bishops to their side, using both persuasion and personal connections. The liberals and Gallicans advocated against papal infallibility, considering it dangerous, as it would further divide the church from the parts of society that respected and demanded liberty. They also believed that papal infallibility would prevent any possible future reunification of the divided Christian churches. The other side, the majority, argued that complete freedom of thought would destroy the church, as the pope would eventually lose his authority.

The press all around Europe reported about the division of the Catholics and their discord during the First Vatican Council. In fact, the bishops of the opposing groups used the press to sway public opinion their way, and they accused each other of betrayal and idolatry. They only managed to discredit the council in the eyes of the public, especially in Germany, where large sectors of the public had negative opinions toward the council. The conservative bishops managed to bring the topic of papal infallibility to the agenda, but that wasn't enough. They also wanted to speed up the council's decision, so they decided to appeal to the pope, who agreed with them and recast the issue into a separate constitution named *De Summo Pontifice*. This four-chapter constitution was immediately given to the bishops for examination.

The debate on this issue lasted from May until July of 1870, and it quickly became obvious that the liberals and Gallicans had no chance to win it. No matter what argument they used against infallibility, the conservatives wouldn't compromise. They had the majority, and they had already decided. But they had to wait for the right time to close the debate. If they did it too soon, public opinion would accuse them of not allowing a proper debate to occur. When the voting time came, 451 bishops voted in favor of papal infallibility, while 88 were against it. Sixty-two bishops voted in favor but demanded some concessions to be made. The initial vote made it clear that the conservatives would win, and sixty of the opposing bishops left the council, as they didn't want to be associated with its approval. The rest were persuaded to vote in favor of the *De*

Summo Pontifice, with only two bishops stubbornly voting against it. In the end, on July 18th, 1870, 535 bishops approved the final text of the constitution.

The council was dismissed for the summer, and plans were made for the next session to start in November. But history prevented this from happening. The pope and the bishops had been so concerned with the issues occurring in the church that they failed to consider the political scene of Europe. French troops, which were stationed in Rome to guarantee the safety of the pope against the Italians who wanted unification, had to retreat when France entered a war with Prussia. United Italy took the opportunity and seized Rome on September 20th, 1870. Pius IX protested the events and proclaimed himself a prisoner in the Vatican, although no one actually prevented him from leaving. The First Vatican Council was not canceled but merely delayed, although the next session would never meet. It was finally closed in the wake of the Second Vatican Council in 1959 by Pope John XXIII.

Nevertheless, those bishops that left the council were pressured to submit to the Vatican decrees, and no serious opposition was mounted against the *De Summo Pontifice* again. The Vatican's definition of infallibility was rejected only in the circles of German universities. Future councils would rectify the exaggerated points of the decree, but by then, many liberals had abandoned their hopes of freeing the Catholic Church. Papal infallibility was proclaimed a dogma, and the Catholic liberals, as well as liberals in general, considered it a serious blow to progress and modernization. But in retrospect, it can be concluded that the church only meant to use infallibility against the state, which could easily infringe upon the church's freedom. Although the state considered itself liberal, in practice, it tended to be very narrow-minded. The state imposed salaries on the clergy, and it planned to impose full control over the national churches. The church was afraid of losing its international reputation, which would promulgate further division. For these reasons, papal infallibility was a necessity.

The Church Responds to the Industrial Revolution

Leo XIII (papacy 1878-1903) succeeded Pius IX, but he was nothing like his predecessor. Although Leo was not fully liberal, he understood that the church needed to accept the fact that the world was in the midst of a change. If it wanted to survive, it, too, had to change. The new pope was a scholar and a diplomat who traveled across Europe and was acquainted with the political and cultural situation of the period. He wanted to elevate the church and start a better relationship with modern secular civilization. To achieve this, he had to update the church intellectually. He instituted a commission to advance the historical research of the Gospels. He also opened the vaults of the Vatican archive to scholars, allowing them a glimpse into the spiritual knowledge previously reserved only for the high clergy.

The Industrial Revolution created new conditions in society, and the church had to respond. The masses suddenly gained the power to decide about the matters that influenced their lives. This was the age of the industrial magnates, with their textile, steel, and coal factories. They dictated the pace of the progress, and it was very fast. By the 1850s, the major cities of Europe were connected by railroads, and the movement of goods and people was revolutionized. Agricultural society was nearing its end, as the people relocated to the cities to work in factories. The population of Europe grew from 188 million to 266 million in just 50 years. By the 1900s, it rose to almost four hundred million, and it is no wonder that mass action and mass suggestion emerged as a political force. The church followed suit, and a new movement was organized as the answer to the rise of the masses: social Catholicism. Its main goal was to allow the church to continue influencing society and keep itself alive and relevant. To do so, the church needed to accept liberal ideas, in particular, the freedom of the press, secularization of the states, civil liberties, democratic constitutions, and the freedom of religion.

Social Catholicism had its path opened by the industrialization of the cities, which created abominable conditions for the factory workers. The majority of the people were poor, lived in slums, and worked fifteen-hour shifts in the production lines to feed their families with only bread and potatoes. The Catholic Church recognized the gravity of the social problems caused by industrialization, and instead of insisting on tradition and blind allegiance, it started working on elevating the major social problems to attract support. Pope Leo XIII was aware that individual charity was no longer sufficient to fight poverty, and he started calling for collective action. But for this to work, there had to be a certain dose of optimism for the future, so the pope employed his bishops across Europe to tackle the workers' problems.

In Italy, Belgium, Germany, and France, the Catholics started leading the way toward solving the problem of poverty. The priests started preaching against liberal capitalism and its unlimited competition, which only caused industrial magnates to earn more money. They advocated for the state's right to intervene against the capitalists. But more important for the common people were the sermons that encouraged them to form workers' associations, which could then force reforms and introduce reasonable working hours, inspections of factories, regulation of child labor, and profit-sharing.

The workers saw hope in the socialists, and socialist political parties started emerging. However, they leaned toward the secular narratives and teachings of Karl Marx (1818–1883), and by 1880, the church no longer had a hold over the people of France. Several Catholic leaders realized that the church needed to assume a new stance and give up its dreams of using the working class to fight against secular socialism. But the young social Catholicism movement was still hated by the mainstream Catholics, who regarded the church as the protector of their private properties and interests. The conservatives in Europe and the United States called for Rome to condemn the labor unions, but socialist Catholics asserted all of their influence on the Roman Curia, which resulted in Rome favoring the labor movements.

In 1891, Pope Leo XIII issued his encyclical *Rerum novarum*. In it, he summarized progressive Catholic thoughts, which supported separate workers' unions, the right of every individual to work, and the right of the people to earn a wage and defend their interests. It also called for insurance against unemployment, sickness, and work-related accidents. This papal encyclical was rightfully referred to as the Magna Carta of social Catholicism. It brought the main social issues of the period into focus and proposed some solutions. But many Catholics chose to ignore the *Rerum novarum*, even though it was proclaimed the official stance of the church. The encyclical also failed to stop the spread of Marxism, but it did assert significant influence on the rising Christian democratic parties and trade unions, both of which would reach their full potential after World War II.

Since the pontificate of Pope Leo XIII, all consecutive popes endorsed his *Rerum novarum*, and they reaffirmed it through several bulls. The Catholic Church has had a significant number of papal statements that keep Catholic thought in touch with modern social issues. The bull *Mater et magistra*, issued by Pope John XXIII in 1961, notes the development of Catholic social thought since its beginning. Various popes put different social issues into focus over time, such as the problems underdeveloped countries face, peace between the nations, and the rise of global poverty. The popes continued to criticize capitalism and the accumulation of wealth in the hands of individuals, as well as the exploitation and oppression of the different social classes. They also insisted on state intervention against capitalist magnates and called all Christians to unite so that a more just social structure could be built. The papal bulls and documents that followed in the footsteps of *Rerum novarum* display the gradual recognition of democracy by the Catholic Church. The Roman Curia recognized democracy as the only form of government capable of tackling the increasing social questions and guaranteeing basic human rights.

Chapter 16 – The Catholic Church's Influence on the World

John Carroll, the first bishop in the United States, circa 1806.
https://en.wikipedia.org/wiki/Catholic_Church_in_the_United_States#/media/File:John_C
arroll_Gilbert_Stuart.jpg

The Catholic Church's expansion, which started in the 16th and 17th centuries with the Jesuit missions, halted during the 18th century. The Age of Reason debilitated the church, and all missionary work was canceled. In some places, the mission was completely stopped, and once it resumed, it had to start from the beginning. In the 19th century, the church experienced a spiritual revival and missionary zeal. The new period of expansion started with elevating enthusiasm. The new epoch started with Pope Gregory XVI (papacy 1831–1846), and many scholars credit him for the expansion of Catholicism. But in truth, it was the new religious orders that sprouted around the church that carried the mission forward. Among these orders were the renewed Jesuits, Dominicans, and Franciscans, but there were also new ones such as the Scheut Fathers and the White Fathers (founded in 1862 and 1868, respectively).

The Catholic Church in Asia

Gregory XVI thought India was the perfect field for the missionaries because the Catholic community at Goa survived during the church's inactivity of the 18th century. The successor of Gregory XVI, Pope Pius IX, was also a zealous missionary, and he expanded the workings of the Catholic missionaries and reached all corners of the world. Under the pontificate of Leo XIII, the Jesuits opened many colleges in India, where they educated the social elite. At that moment, India already had twenty bishops. By 1958, 75 percent of Catholics in India were native people, and the number of bishops climbed to seventy-seven, of which forty-five were Indians. Five years later, the number of Christians in India climbed to six million. They opened and worked in various colleges, hospitals, schools, and homes for the elderly. Thus, the church managed to influence all aspects of life in India. The statistics of 2011 estimated that there are around twenty million Catholics in India, but they represent only 1.5 percent of the total population.

China, the most populated country in the world, was fascinated with Christian missionaries. There, the spread of Christianity started in the 17th century, but the church founded by Matteo Ricci and his followers fell into disuse during the 18th century. Toward the middle of the 19th century, the mission in China revived, but it now had competition, as Protestants sent their missionaries as well. Nevertheless, by the 1890s, China had around half a million Catholics and around 369 native priests. But the mission went through a very difficult time when the colonial powers invaded China. The population was now divided between the British, French, and Portuguese spheres of influence, but this wasn't as problematic as the First Sino-Japanese War (1894–1895) and the Boxer Rebellion (1899–1901). The old Confucian monarchy of China was overthrown, and the country entered the 20th century in violence and confusion.

At the beginning of the 20th century, a Western-style republic was born, and the traditional Chinese religions, such as Confucianism, Taoism, and Buddhism, started declining. This opened the way for the Catholics and Protestants to assert their influence, and many of the natives were willing to listen to the new Christian teachings. By 1922, the Roman Catholics numbered over two million, though soon enough, the Chinese government proclaimed Christianity an imperialistic tool. Communism took over, and religion itself was made obsolete. Despite this, the Catholic Church continued to prosper until 1937, which was when Japan attacked again. Their numbers continuously grew, and after World War II, there were twenty archdioceses and seventy-nine dioceses in China; there was also one archbishopric of Peking, where Cardinal Thomas Tien presided. Still, the Catholics didn't make even 1 percent of the whole population of China.

The communist takeover of the country was finished by 1950, and with it came a difficult period for Christianity in China. All foreign missions were canceled, and missionaries were either imprisoned or expelled from communist China. However, Catholicism was never officially banned. The communist leader, Mao Zedong (1893–1976), wanted to cut the ties the Chinese Catholics had with the foreigners, and for this purpose, the Catholic Patriotic Church was founded in 1958. This church was independent of Rome, so the papacy has no records of how many clergymen it had or how many people decided to join it.

In Japan, Christianity has been present since 1549 through the works of Francis Xavier. The church made great progress during its first century of existence on Japanese soil, and although the Jesuits and Franciscans were often persecuted there, they made tremendous changes. But Shogun Hideyoshi, the imperial regent and national hero who united Japan, decided to exterminate Christianity. In 1638, the Christians of Shimabara Peninsula revolted, which led to the massacre of thirty-five thousand people. All signs of Christianity were obliterated by Shogun Hideyoshi's government. For the next two centuries, Japan was completely disconnected from the rest of the world, and no foreigner was allowed to step on the island.

The renewed mission in Japan only started in 1853 when Commodore Matthew Perry of the United States visited the island nation and signed a trade and friendship treaty. In 1855, the first missionaries came to Japan and began the evangelization of the nation. These first missionaries experienced something close to a miracle in their initial travels through Japan. The missionary chapel at Nagasaki received a band of Japanese visitors who acted extremely pious and respectful. Father Petitjean asked them who they were and where they came from, only to learn that they were Christians who managed to preserve their faith for two centuries by hiding and secretly preaching. They had no priest to lead them, but they managed to preserve the essentials of Christianity: baptism, consolation of the dying, and Sunday Mass. Other hidden Christian communities were discovered in the mountains and caves around Nagasaki, numbering around ten thousand in total.

But practicing Christianity was still considered illegal under Japanese law, and once the government learned of their existence, they started persecuting them. Many crypto-Christians were forced into exile or were simply executed. When the world press started reporting about the persecutions of crypto-Christians in Japan, the government finally agreed to issue a new constitution in 1889, by which all people were granted complete religious freedom. In 1891, Pope Leo XIII started the Japanese hierarchy of the church with the archbishopric in Tokyo, which numbered around forty-five thousand Catholics. But the first native bishop in Japan only appeared in 1927 during the pontificate of Pius XI. A Japanese archbishop of Tokyo was appointed in 1936, and in 1940, the Japanese episcopate was handed over to the natives.

Christianity in Japan suffered during World War II, as many churches were destroyed, and many people perished. The nuclear attack on Nagasaki killed 64,000 people, of which 8,500 were Catholics. After the war, Japan was left in ruins and with a dying economy. The government abolished the old Shinto religion, and many people had nowhere to turn to for spiritual leadership but Christianity. This accelerated the rate of conversion, but the Protestants received more attention than the Catholics. By 2014, there were 440,000 Catholics and twice that many Protestants in Japan.

Other Asian countries had successful Christian missions too. In Korea, Christianity took root immediately after World War II. The Catholic population grew extremely fast, as missionaries from Mexico, the United States, and Europe rushed to the country. Many Koreans studied abroad after the war, and when they returned to their country, they shared their modern view of the world and their newly acquired faith. Many of these returnees had not only been converted abroad but also became priests. Unfortunately, the Park regime in Korea wasn't fond of Catholicism, especially those who advocated social changes. In 1974, Daniel Tji Hak-Soun (1921–1993), the bishop of Wonju, was arrested and sentenced to fifteen years of prison because he denounced the Yushin constitution, which he believed violated basic human rights. The government used this constitution to keep the Park regime in power. Catholics all over Korea, numbering around 800,000, demanded Daniel's release. They organized massive protests and forced the government to release Bishop Tji after spending only one year in prison.

In Indonesia, the Sukarno autocratic government was overthrown in 1966, which opened the way for the Christian missions. Recent numbers display that there are around 20.2 million Protestants and 8.3 million Catholics in Indonesia. The largest daily newspaper in Indonesia is run by Catholics, and the faith seems to be the most appealing to the social elite and the intellectuals. Pakistan, Taiwan, Hong Kong, Thailand, Burma, Malaysia, and Ceylon each have a Catholic community of at least 300,000 members. In Vietnam, there are around seven million Catholics. The Philippines has the most Catholics, around eighty-four million people, which is 85 percent of the total population.

The Catholic Church in Africa

Just like in Asia, the mission in Africa practically stopped during the 18th century. Napoleon tried to establish churches in the coastal regions, and although they took root, they never bloomed. In 1849, an explorer and Protestant missionary from Scotland, David Livingston (1813–1873), opened the way to inner Africa. He proved that a white man could survive the harsh conditions of the continent, and many Christian missionaries became interested in bringing the faith to the African territories south of the Sahara Desert.

The most important Catholic missionary in Africa was Charles Lavigerie (1825–1892), the former bishop of Nancy, France. He became archbishop of Algiers in 1867, where he planned to make a base for the conversion of the African continent. The next year, he founded the Society of Missionaries of Africa, also known as the White Fathers. At first, he tried to reinforce Catholicism in mostly Muslim coastal regions, but seeing this as impossible, he sent his men to equatorial Uganda, where the Protestant missionaries had already prepared the grounds for conversion.

Mutesa I, the king of Buganda (a kingdom within Uganda), didn't want anything to do with the foreigners, and he decided to play the Muslims, Protestants, and the Catholics against each other so they would leave his people alone. Mwanga II, the next king, displayed favoritism for the Catholics, but this turned out to be a pretense. He was a bloodthirsty tyrant, and he burned all of the Catholic and Protestant missionaries who refused his homosexual advances alive. But politics played a final role in Mwanga's reign, as he was dethroned by the British, who then crowned his brother. But Mwanga approached and made a deal with the British East African Company, and in 1889, he resumed his reign. The company also forced him to convert to Christianity.

The ordinary people of Africa proved to be receptive to the Christian faith. They were curious about the religion, and they liked Christian stories and the Gospels. The White Fathers preached to Ugandans, and by the end of World War I, they had around fifteen thousand converts. However, the Catholic mission was even more successful in Belgian Congo, now the Democratic Republic of the Congo. Catholic missionaries in Congo enjoyed the privileges granted to them by the Belgian government, and they flourished in this African country. Through the works of the White Fathers, by 1959, the Catholics made up around 36 percent of the total population. Today, Christians of all denominations number over 95 percent of the population. In neighboring Rwanda and Burundi, the majority of the population is Roman Catholic.

Catholicism failed to penetrate South Africa, where the British rooted themselves. Other African countries outside of the Muslim belt proved to be very receptive to Christianity and the Catholic Church. In Nigeria, the Christian community is ever-growing, with both Protestants and Catholics dominating its education system, though the country remains split between Christians and Muslims. Everywhere in Africa, Christianity is on the rise, and most of the Christian people belong to the Roman Catholic Church, closely followed by the Eastern Catholic Church.

But the church in Africa still faces some problems. The missionaries failed to install Christianity into African cultures and traditions, and many people would still rather turn to Islam. Because Christianity was preached only in its European form, many Africans created a hybrid form of the faith and started various African Christian sects.

The Catholic Church in the Americas

The Catholic Church in the United States was incredibly successful during the 19th century. The Catholic immigrants from Poland, Ireland, Italy, and Germany filled the ranks of the church in the United States and even surpassed its national growth. The American bishops managed to integrate these newly arrived immigrants into the already existing Catholic community and provide them with the best schools and hospitals. Catholics all around the world could only envy American progress.

But the first Catholic missionaries in America had to go through a period of hardship and constant trial to plant the seeds of faith in the new continent. In the 17th century, the Jesuits, Franciscans, and Capuchins rushed to save the souls of the Native Americans. However, they were often greeted by death, and they had to fight for their survival and the right to build little Christian churches that would become the nucleus of Catholic life and their parishes.

Hundreds of Catholic priests evangelized the Native Americans, and among them, two names stand out: Junipero Serra of the Franciscans and Father Eusebio Kino of the Jesuits. Both of them worked in the Spanish-held territories of Florida and California. To the north was the French area, where the Jesuit Père Jacques Marquette and Isaac Jogues worked with many tribes.

In the thirteen British colonies, the Catholics didn't come with a mission in mind. They were running from persecution, just like the Puritans and the Quakers. The Catholics were well received in Maryland, which was founded by the baron of Baltimore, George Calvert, as a haven for all Christians. In Pennsylvania, which was founded by the Quakers, liberal politics welcomed the Catholics to settle. In 1776, both in Maryland and in Pennsylvania, the Catholics were given religious freedom and independence. Until then, they were ruled by the apostolic residence in London. The Roman Curia finally granted the United States their bishop, John Carroll, in 1789. He laid the grounds for the development and expansion of the Catholic Church in the United States.

Another prominent name in early United States Catholic history was the bishop of Charleston, South Carolina, John England (1786–1842). Anxious and enthusiastic, England jumped on every opportunity to preach to the non-Catholics. He even held a two-hour-long speech in front of Congress, which was the triumph of his career. But England was different from other Catholic preachers because he understood that the church needed to adapt to the American spirit to survive in the new continent. He combined clergy and laity into a form of church government, and they worked together to promulgate the diocese's policies. Unfortunately, this democratic setup was far ahead of its time, and it didn't survive after his death.

John England was also responsible for the foundation of the Baltimore ecclesiastical councils, which were held between 1829 and 1884. American bishops gathered in this council to discuss and decide how to lead the way throughout the many crises the church experienced in the New World. Under their leadership, the dioceses flourished, and the American Catholic Church kept pace with the development of American society, culture, politics, and industry. By the time of the First Plenary Council of Baltimore, held in 1852, six archbishoprics were already fully functional: Baltimore, Portland, St. Louis, New Orleans, Cincinnati, and New York. The number of archbishoprics grew to eleven by the time of the Second Plenary Council in 1884, with the addition of Santa Fe, Milwaukee, Philadelphia, Boston, and Chicago.

Immigrants started arriving in the United States, and they swelled the numbers of the Catholic population. The Catholics were almost invisible at the start of North American colonization, but they became the largest religious denomination by 1850. Their growth continued, as Catholic immigrants poured into the country from Ireland, Germany, and especially Italy and Poland up until 1920.

But culturally, the United States was dominated by the Protestants, who became hostile toward the influx of Catholics. The Catholic Church was forced to create a world of its own and assume a defensive stance in the face of hostility. Central to this defense was the foundation of parochial schools. Public schools were heavily influenced by the Protestants, as the only Bible allowed was the Protestant version. When the Catholics protested and tried to push for the acceptance of the Catholic Bible, they were met with harsh resistance. So, they started opening their own schools in which children would be taught only the Catholic faith. By 1840, around two hundred parochial schools were operating across the United States. They were the nucleus of what would later become a network of private schools.

The immigration laws of the 1920s brought an end to the influx of immigrants, and the Catholic numbers ceased rising. Its rate of growth was now practically the same as that of the Protestants. By 1950, the Protestants constituted 33.8 percent of the total population of the United States, while the Catholics had 18.9 percent. But by then, the Catholic Church in the United States had become an American institution. Although it had its ups and downs and several major issues that threatened internal division, the church survived and started dominating the American world. During the presidential elections of 1960, the United States gained its first Catholic president, John F. Kennedy. Pope John XXIII would soon call the Second Council of Vatican, an event that would propel American Catholicism into the new era.

Chapter 17 – The Church in Modern Times

Vatican relief packages being delivered to prisoners of war in Italy, 1917.
https://en.wikipedia.org/wiki/Pope_Benedict_XV#/media/File:Pio1917.jpg

The first pope elected at the beginning of the 20th century was Pius X (papacy 1903-1914). Even as a pope, Pius loved his work as a priest, and he continued saying Mass, hearing confessions, and catechizing children. He was known for his warm humor and gentleness, and people all around the world loved him. His most important work as the pope reflected his love for priestly work. In a decree he issued in 1903, he reformed the sacred Mass and included music in it so that it could be performed in the most dignified manner. Another decree he issued urged the people to partake of communion and the early baptism of their children. But his biggest project was the codification of the canon law, although it was only promulgated in 1917 during the pontificate of Benedict XV.

Pius X had no interest in modernizing the church so it could fit the political and cultural image of the modern world. His view of contemporary politics, culture, and industry was mostly negative. He didn't care for democracy, which started being the political trend. He believed democracy was a violation of the natural hierarchy of society, and he often warned the Catholics to be wary of democracy. During his pontificate, many Christian democratic societies and political parties were closed or worked underground.

One aspect of the church's relationship with the modern world irked Pius X and made him react with vigor. France abrogated the concordat signed by Napoleon and Pope Pius VII in 1905 and tried to subdue the church and make it financially dependent on the state. The pope warned the French bishop that it would be better if the church relied on its own riches and rejected the state's financial aid. He also reminded the clergy that the church's riches were in its tradition, spirituality, and devotion, not in materialistic things. Pope Pius X couldn't even imagine that by ordering the French bishops to reject financial ties with the state, he would open the way for the church's renewal, which would lead to the Second Vatican Council.

The Popes of the World Wars

Pius X's successor was Benedict XV (papacy 1914–1922), and he started his pontificate when Europe was plunged into the First World War. Benedict was elected because he had the spirit of a peacemaker, and he didn't disappoint his Catholic followers. Peace and reconciliations were the main goals of his pontificate. But first, he needed to reconcile the church, which was violently divided by the anti-modernists of Pius X. During his pontificate, the religious organizations that sought the modernization of the church were allowed to operate without restrictions.

But Benedict's role as a peacemaker for the powers involved in the Great War was much harder. He needed to employ all of his diplomatic powers to be able to navigate the subtle political currents of a Europe in conflict. For Benedict XV, there was no justification for the war. He was against the conflict with all his being, morally and intellectually. Nevertheless, he never openly condemned the war because he didn't want to divide the Catholics, as there were still those who were emotionally not ready to accept the anti-war sentiment. All he could do was send appeals to both sides, begging them to end the madness and useless killing. In August 1917, he issued his famous (though futile) "Note to the Heads of State at War." This note was the pope's peace plan, in which he listed seven proposals on how to end the hostilities. He also called for disarmament and the establishment of political arbitration, which would include international sanctions.

Benedict's unambiguous condemnation of the war, as well as the fact that he refused to take sides, was misinterpreted by the participants. They all wanted the pope to condemn the other side. The press made a villain out of the pope, and he was not invited to join the Paris Peace Conference. Benedict's contemporaries were unable to recognize his true intentions as a peacemaker. Interestingly enough, United States President Woodrow Wilson was the first to decline the "Note to the Heads of State at War," even though he later included most of the seven peace proposals into his Fourteen Points, which were used as a plan to end World War I. The value of Benedict's diplomatic efforts to end the war was recognized only after his death, and he served as a model to Pius XII, whose pontificate was during World War II.

Benedict XV didn't only use his diplomatic skills to relieve the war-torn world. He was also never able to refuse charity, and during his pontificate, the Vatican's treasury was almost emptied, as he redirected the funds to help the poor, sick, and starving. From the beginning of the war, he acted as a medium between the warring parties wishing to exchange prisoners, wounded soldiers, and even civilians. He also personally financed care packages for the prisoners of war on both sides. The pope was especially worried about the children, and most of the Vatican's funds were spent to feed the children in German-occupied Belgium, Poland, Montenegro, Lithuania, Russia, and Syria. He had to appeal to the people and clergy of the United States to help him in his efforts to save these children. Upon his death, the Vatican had barely enough money to cover the expenses of the conclave, the meeting of the cardinals to elect the new pope.

Benedict's successor was Pius XI (papacy 1922–1939), who focused his pontificate on the reconciliation of the church and Italy, a conflict that had lasted since the conquest of the Papal States in 1870. When giving his first papal benediction, Pope Pius XI appeared on the balcony of St. Peter's Basilica, something no pope did after 1846. At that moment, Italy was digging a grave for democracy by following Benito Mussolini's fascism. Pius XI thought that Italy needed a strong figure such as Mussolini, and he paved the way for his victory by withdrawing the Vatican's support to the Catholic Popular Party. To show his gratitude, Mussolini signed the Lateran Concordat and the Vatican Treaty in 1929, by which the pope gave up his claim over the Papal States but received a generous sum of money and complete control over Vatican City.

The Lateran Concordat made Roman Catholicism the official religion of Italy and imposed Catholic religious teachings in the secular state schools.

In other states of Europe, dictators came to power, and Pius XI didn't hesitate to make deals with them. For this, he gladly sacrificed Catholic political parties. However, the situation in Germany was more complicated, as Adolf Hitler was condemned by the German bishops even before he came to power. But in 1933, once he assumed power, Hitler declared that he felt both Catholic and Protestant churches were pivotal for the preservation of German national heritage. He promised the churches would have full respect for their freedoms, but in turn, they had to support his efforts to purify the nation and public life, even if it meant open conflict. The German bishops felt compelled and withdrew their previous condemnation of Hitler. Later the same year, the Vatican signed a concordat with Hitler that would guarantee religious freedom for the Catholic Church.

In truth, Pius XI had no political preferences toward fascism, and he used pragmatism to secure the well-being of the Catholic Church. He condemned fascism when the Italian troops started their campaign in Ethiopia. Still, Pius did rule in the fashion of the medieval popes, and he claimed complete sovereignty over his domain, the church. He was a tyrant and didn't allow anyone to challenge his orders and decisions. He made all the calls alone, and he took no advice from his cardinals. His presence was strong and demanded attention. Even Hermann Göring, the second in command of Nazi Germany, admitted he was awed when in the presence of Pope Pius XI.

But this attitude served Pius well once Mussolini tried to suppress Catholic organizations in Italy. The pope managed to scare the dictator and force him to back down. When Hitler tried to do the same, Pius met the challenge and published his *Mit Brennender Sorge*, an encyclical in which he finally dared to criticize and condemn Nazism. However, all of his further actions against fascism and Nazism in Italy and Germany were prevented by his sudden death in 1939.

The next pope had previously served Pius XI as his secretary of state, Pius XII (papacy 1939–1958). He was a well-traveled diplomat, and the cardinals chose him because a diplomat was needed in a world that would soon be engulfed in yet another world war. The war came only two weeks after Pius XII was coronated as pope when Hitler sent tanks to Czechoslovakia. Pius rushed to put his diplomatic skills to good use and try to prevent a catastrophe. He even acted as an intermediary between the Allied Powers and the resistance forces in the underground German political scene. But when Italy joined the war, Pius realized the Vatican could be seen as part of the Allies, and he was afraid his sacred city would be attacked. The pope had to play the role of a neutral observer to avoid an attack. And even when the war took a course that ensured an Allied victory, the pope didn't rush to join them. He was afraid communism would prevail among the Allies, and if there was something he hated more than Nazism, it was communism. Pius XI worked in favor of a negotiated peace that would prevent the Soviet Union from occupying the whole of Germany.

The end of the war brought an economic boom to Italy. Many tourists, mainly from the United States, rushed to Rome and the Vatican. The Holy See took its share of the wealth that the pilgrims left behind and enriched its newly opened bank. The pope himself gave daily speeches from his balcony, addressing pilgrims and blessing all visitors. But communism remained a threat after the war, and the pope decided to align the Catholic Church more closely to Western democracy. Pius XII used all of the means at his disposal to prevent communism from reaching Italy and Rome, and in 1949, he issued a decree by which all Catholics who belonged to the Communist Party were excommunicated. He also tried to influence the Democratic Party of Italy to ban communism.

The Second Vatican Council

The successor of Pope Pius XII, John XXIII (papacy 1958–1963), proved to be a completely different pope. He loved life, people, and simplicity, and he was not afraid to show it. He loved making jokes, visiting prisons and hospitals, and speaking to everyone who sought him. He didn't give a thought to papal etiquette, and he often invited his friends for dinner and walked the streets of Rome, addressing the common people. He was the first pope since the dawn of time to remind the people he was only a human. For this, he was loved and respected by many, even non-Christians, whom he invited to the Vatican and spoke to them as equals.

John XXIII remains remembered in history as the pope who opened up a dialogue with the world. He issued two encyclicals: *Pacem in terris* and *Mater et magistra*, by which he addressed all the people of the earth and called them to work together and build a better world. He reversed the anti-communist policies of his predecessors and sought to achieve a peaceful relationship with the communists. But the Curia remained predominantly conservative, and all the goodwill of Pope John could have easily perished after his death if he did not call the famous Second Vatican Council in 1962. This council gathered bishops from around the world in a heart-to-heart conversation with humanity, during which many spiritual issues of the period were resolved.

Pope John's initial idea for this council was to work on the unification of all Christians. But the main problem the council needed to address was the reform of the old, stubbornly traditional, and anti-modernist church so it could meet the spiritual needs of the people who lived in an ever-changing world. After all, the post-war era propelled humanity into the future, with scientific, technological, cultural, political, and social developments changing life for so many people. The church, on the other hand, felt left behind. Nevertheless, the cardinals remained reluctant to agree that change was needed. Once the pope announced his intention to call a council, they felt as if he called for a revolution. The cardinals devised a strategy by which they would ensure their control over the council and not allow the pope to assert his influence.

At first, the cardinals succeeded in their intentions, and they secured key positions on the commissions that drew up the scheme for the council. Bishops around the world sent their proposals for what should be addressed during the council, and the commission chose seventy. These proposals touched upon many subjects, such as ecclesiastical benefices, reincarnation, spiritualism, anathemas, and the revelation. The cardinals hoped everything would go smoothly and that the council would approve of the proposals and end quickly.

The council opened on October 11th, 1962, and around 2,500 bishops attended it, with numerous nuns, clergy, auditors, and laymen (and women) observing it. As the pope closed the first meeting on the first day of the council, he addressed the gathered people and made sure it was clear that he had no associations with the narrow-minded view of the council. The pope had an optimistic view of the council and expressed his hopes that the church would finally align itself with the modern world. He also warned the bishops of the danger of endless and sterile academic discussions and urged them to find meaningful and positive ways in which they could take action to bring about the church's reform.

To achieve what the pope wished, the bishops needed to remove the Curia's power over the council and take stronger positions in the commission. The power struggle began, and although the Curia had a head-start with the already prepared schemata and a list of candidates for the commission, the bishops managed to defeat them. The men elected for the commission were truly independent of the Curia's grasp, and they represented the worldviews of various episcopates. Their first task was to revise the seventy proposals and draft documents that the Curia had already prepared. They rewrote sixty-nine of these documents since they were already outdated. The one proposal that was to open to discussion was the reform of the liturgy, and the first debate proved that the bishops had a progressive view. This was good news for the pope, and he hoped the bishops would display such enthusiasm for other points of reform.

The council was divided among the liberal and conservative bishops, but unlike during the First Vatican Council, the liberals had the majority. During the four years of council meetings, these two groups often quarreled and caused major crises. Pope John XXIII intervened during the first crisis, which arose with the question of revelation, one of the major doctrines of the church. To prevent discord, the pope ordered the schema to be redrafted so it could be in the spirit of open dialogue. The first recess was called on December 8th, 1962, and before the council could reconvene, Pope John died.

Many bishops believed another crisis would emerge, as no one could guarantee that the next pope would be progressive as John. They feared his successor would hurry to close the council without establishing the points on which the church would be reformed. But that wasn't the case. The next pope was Paul VI (papacy 1963–1978), who continued in the spirit of his predecessor. The next session of the Second Vatican Council was opened on September 29th, 1963, and the pope used the opening session to reassure the bishops that the council's main goal was the reform of the church, unity with all Christians, and the continuation of the dialogue with the world.

The topics of these sessions revolved around ecumenism, anti-Semitism, modern communications, and religious freedoms. On all points, the council displayed enormous enthusiasm, positivity, and progress. During the third session, the church finally touched on the topic of its relation to the modern world, and matters such as marital morality and artificial insemination were discussed. But before the bishops could discuss such topics, they needed to decide the Catholic position in the world and renounce the *Syllabus of Errors*, which claimed that the Catholic Church should have primacy in all states and that other religions should be merely tolerated. The church finally agreed to have an equal status with the other religions, though this discussion wasn't smooth. Many conservative bishops used papal primacy as an excuse to keep the Catholic Church in a privileged position.

The fourth and final session of the council opened on September 14th, 1965, and it dealt with the final chapter of the schema on the church and its relation to the modern world, "The Community of Nations and the Building Up of Peace." At the same time, Pope Paul VI attended the United Nations to advocate for peace, and his speech was well received. Other major topics the council discussed were the question of Jews, who were no longer considered responsible for the death of Jesus Christ, and reconciliation with the Eastern Orthodox Church. At the end of the council, Pope Paul VI expressed regret on behalf of all Catholics for the events that caused the Great Schism in 1054, and Patriarch Athenagoras did the same in Istanbul.

To maintain the reform of the Catholic Church, Pope Paul VI established the Synod of Bishops, which became a permanent institution and the advisory body to the papacy. They were to meet periodically and discuss major issues of the Catholic faith in the modern world. Paul also reformed the Roman Curia by reducing its bureaucracy and including more non-Italians. The Second Vatican Council caused a tidal wave of change throughout the Catholic world and uprooted many Catholics by shaking their firm beliefs in tradition, nationality, and community. The church was becoming modern, and its followers had to accept it, whether they liked it or not. However, most Catholics in the world accepted the changes without raising major issues, as humanity was aware of the necessities of the times.

Contemporary Popes

Pope Paul's successor was John Paul I, the first pope in the history of Catholicism to assume two names. He did it because he couldn't deny the influence that his immediate predecessors had on him, and he wanted to show his respect for both John XXIII and Paul VI. John Paul had great plans and was enthusiastic about the reforms that the church was experiencing. Unfortunately, his pontificate lasted for only one month, from August 26th until September 28th, 1978. The next pope assumed the same name in his honor and started his pontificate as John Paul II (papacy 1978–2005). He came from Poland, which made him the first non-Italian pope elected since the 16th century.

John Paul II was the first pope in history to teach the *Theology of the Body*, a series of lectures on human sexuality. Although this might have been seen as a good step toward the reformation of the church and its progressivity, his teachings proved to be quite conservative. He preached against homosexuality, abortion, and even contraceptives. But the main goal of the *Theology of the Body* was to explore the human body as a tool by which people can serve God. He focuses more on marriage, celibacy, and the body's purity than on the controversial topics of LBTQ rights and contraception.

Pope John Paul proved to be more progressive when it came to matters of science. He acknowledged the research done by many evolutionists and agreed to personally enforce the theory of evolution. However, he had to make one exception, the human soul. Though he admitted the human body originated from the living material that had already existed on earth, human souls were created by God and were, therefore, divine.

John Paul II was a spiritual inspiration for the downfall of communism in Central and Eastern Europe. His guidance in the murky waters of delicate politics can be summed up in his own words: "Do not be afraid." But it wasn't only his spiritual leadership and prayers that were the catalyst for the solidarity and union of the communist world. He also used the Vatican Bank to fund the cause and many solidarity movements that fought against communism. Even the last leader of the Soviet Union expressed his belief that the Iron Curtain, which divided Europe, wouldn't have fallen without the efforts of John Paul II. US President George W. Bush awarded the pope with the Presidential Medal of Freedom for inspiring people to bring communism and tyranny down.

For his efforts, in 1981, the pope was shot by a Turkish fascist, Mehmet Ağca, a member of the far-right military organization known as the Grey Wolves. He survived the assassination attempt, but another attempt on his life was made the very next year. In Portugal, a man stabbed the pope with a knife. Although John Paul was injured, he hid his non-life-threatening wound and continued with the procession in Fatima. This attack was conducted by an angry priest who didn't like the reforms of the church established during the Second Vatican Council.

John Paul II died on April 2nd, 2005. His successor was Pope Benedict XVI (papacy 2005-2013), the first pope to resign of his free will since Gregory XII in 1415. Although he started his career as a liberal theologian, he adopted conservative views later in life and kept them during his pontificate. He didn't like the increasing secularization of the Western world, and he advocated the return to the fundamental values of the church. Even though a conservative, he refrained from changing the Roman Curia and the major points of the Second Vatican Council to what they had been beforehand. The changes he did introduce were very modest and mostly consisted of merging some of the offices. He resigned on February 28th, 2013, expressing his bodily and mental weakness, which he believed would only hinder his ability to lead the church.

Conclusion

As the oldest institution of the Western world, the Catholic Church had many difficulties finding common ground with the secular world. Through the ages, it expressed a desire to dominate, control, and rule over the people, both in temporal and secular matters. But if its history is studied carefully, it becomes obvious that the church went a long way to accommodate the demands of the different historical periods. The Catholics believe their church was founded by no other than Jesus Christ, and they draw their spirit from the ancient period and the tradition of the early centuries. The popes felt it was their duty to preserve the purity of the faith, and the only way they knew how to do that was through the preservation of the old doctrines, dogmas, and traditions.

In modern times, the Catholic Church underwent many changes. Although many people feel as if the church will never break free from its medieval thought, the contemporary popes are liberal, democratic, and modern. The current pope, Francis (papacy 2013-ongoing), even admitted he was just a man and had no right to deprive the LGBTQ people of their faith if they seek it. The papacy understands the need to adjust to the modern world, not just to secure the existence of the faith but to be able to keep the church's dominance over the spiritual lives of its followers.

Changes have been ongoing since the Council of Trent. The world is ever progressing, and so, the church must follow. The Renaissance and the Enlightenment saw the aristocrats try to break off from the conservative church but only after the French Revolution. The first in line to reform the church after the revolution was the liberal Catholics, who started some of the first Christian political parties and expanded the reform of the church onto the secular states.

Although it seemed as if the First Vatican Council would revert all of the implemented changes, it did not happen. Pope Pius IX was just one man, and his *Syllabus of Errors* couldn't last for long. The many wars that started in Europe disrupted the efforts of the Roman Curia to revert to the conservative way. The Franco-Prussian War allowed the Italians to take over the Papal States and unify their country under a single, secular rule. Many Western European states were inspired by the Italians' unity and finally felt free of the ultramontanism imposed on them by the papacy of Pius IX.

The world wars brought about a different effort in regards to the church. The world was suffering, and the popes wouldn't allow it. The true Christian spirit was revived during the Second Vatican Council, which understood that peacemaking needed to be the priority. It seems that since the world wars, the Catholic Church has turned toward their charity and diplomatic work to relieve the world from the horrors of military conflicts. The modern popes use their education and their connection with the people to give inspiring speeches during various world summits and even before the United Nations. They took it upon themselves to wrestle communism and end its grip over Central and Eastern Europe. They preach peace for the Middle East and advocate the end of hunger in African states. The church finally gave up on its dream to dominate the lives of nations and their rulers and accepted the more humble but crucial role of a spiritual and moral leader.

Here's another book by Captivating History that you might like

Free Bonus from Captivating History
(Available for a Limited time)

Hi History Lovers!

Now you have a chance to join our exclusive history list so you can get your first history ebook for free as well as discounts and a potential to get more history books for free! Simply visit the link below to join.

Captivatinghistory.com/ebook

Also, make sure to follow us on Facebook, Twitter and Youtube by searching for Captivating History.

References

Alberigo, G., & Komonchak, J. A. (2006). *History of Vatican II.* Maryknoll, NY: Orbis.

Alvarez, D. J. (2011). *The Pope's Soldiers: A Military History of the Modern Vatican.* Lawrence, Kan.: University Press of Kansas.

Bainton, R. H. (1966). *The History of Christianity.* London: Reprint Society London.

Bornkamm, G. (1995). *Jesus of Nazareth.* Minneapolis: Fortress Press.

Bourmaud, D. (2006). *One Hundred Years of Modernism: A History of Modernism, Aristotle to the Second Vatican Council.* Kansas City, MO: Angelus Press.

Broderick, R. C. (1987). *The Catholic Encyclopedia.* Nashville, TN: Thomas Nelson.

Brown, P. (1982). *Society and the Holy in Late Antiquity.* Berkeley: Univ. of Calif. Pr.

Cadoux, C. J. (1955). *The Early Church and the World: A History of the Christian Attitude to Pagan Society and the State Down to the Time of Constantinus.* Edinburgh: T. & T. Clark.

Duchensne, L. M., & Jenkins, C. (1922). *Early History of the Christian Church.* New York: Longmans, Green.

Eusebius, & Lake, K. (1980). *The Ecclesiastical History.* London.

Küng, H. (2003). *The Catholic Church: A Short History.* New York: Modern Library.

Laporte, J. (1982). *The Role of Women in Early Christianity.* New York: Mellen Press.

Logan, F. D. (2013). *A History of the Church in the Middle Ages.* London: Routledge.

New Catholic Encyclopedia. (2003). Detroit, MI: Gale Group in association with the Catholic University of America.

Pastor, L. (1978). *The History of the Popes from the Close of the Middle Ages.* Wilmington, NC: Consortium.

Petry, R. C., & Manschreck, C. L. (1990). *A History of Christianity: Readings in the History of the Church.* Grand Rapids, MI: Baker.

Rasmussen, M. (2005). *The Catholic Church: The First 2,000 Years: A Popular Survey and Study Guide to Church History.* San Francisco: Ignatius Press.

R. V. Sellers. *Council of Chalcedon*, p. 211. (London: S.P.C.K., 1961)

Straus, B. R. (1992). *The Catholic Church.* New York, NY: Hippocrene Books

Urban, L. (1995). *A Short History of Christian Thought.* New York: Oxford University Press.

Walls, A. F. (2000). *The Missionary Movement in Christian History: Studies in the Transmission of Faith.* Maryknoll, NY: Orbis Books.

Wilson, P. H. (2016). *Heart of Europe: A History of the Holy Roman Empire.* Cambridge, MA: The Belknap Press of Harvard University Press.

Made in the USA
Middletown, DE
06 April 2024

52698065R00119